Rossiter Johnson

Comedy

Rossiter Johnson

Comedy

ISBN/EAN: 9783337004767

Printed in Europe, USA, Canada, Australia, Japan

Cover: Foto ©Thomas Meinert / pixelio.de

More available books at **www.hansebooks.com**

LITTLE CLASSICS.

"A series of exquisitely printed little volumes in flexible binding and red edges, which gather up the very choicest things in our literature in the way of short tales and sketches." — Buffalo Courier.

The Prose Series includes 12 volumes, as follows:

EXILE.	*ROMANCE.*
INTELLECT.	*MYSTERY.*
TRAGEDY.	*COMEDY.*
LIFE.	*CHILDHOOD.*
LAUGHTER.	*HEROISM.*
LOVE.	*FORTUNE.*

Tastefully bound. Price, $1.00 each.

"No more delightful reading can be conceived than the polished and attractive papers that are selected for this series." — *Boston Gazette.*

"Too much praise cannot be accorded the projectors of this work. It lays, for a very small sum, the cream of the best writers before the reader of average means. It usually happens that very few, except professional people and scholars, care to read all that even the most famous men have written. They want his best work, — the one people talk most about, — and when they have read that they are satisfied." — *N. Y. Commercial Adv.*

⁂ For sale by Booksellers. Sent, post-paid, on receipt of price by the Publishers,

JAMES R. OSGOOD & CO., Boston.

Ninth Volume.

LITTLE CLASSICS.

EDITED BY

ROSSITER JOHNSON.

COMEDY.

BARNY O'REIRDON THE NAVIGATOR. — HAGGAD-BEN-AHAB THE TRAVELLER. BLUEBEARD'S GHOST. — THE PICNIC PARTY. — FATHER TOM AND THE POPE. — JOHNNY DARBYSHIRE. — THE GRIDIRON. — THE BOX TUNNEL.

BOSTON:
JAMES R. OSGOOD AND COMPANY,
Late Ticknor & Fields, and Fields, Osgood, & Co.
1875.

UNIVERSITY PRESS: WELCH, BIGELOW, & CO.,
CAMBRIDGE.

CONTENTS.

		PAGE
BARNY O'REIRDON THE NAVIGATOR	*Samuel Lover* . .	7
HADDAD-BEN-AHAB THE TRAVELLER	*John Galt* . . .	58
BLUEBEARD'S GHOST	*Wm. M. Thackeray* .	67
THE PICNIC PARTY	*Horace Smith* . .	102
FATHER TOM AND THE POPE . .	*Samuel Ferguson* .	131
JOHNNY DARBYSHIRE	*William Howitt* .	168
THE GRIDIRON	*Samuel Lover* . .	206
THE BOX TUNNEL	*Charles Reade* . .	217

BARNY O'REIRDON THE NAVIGATOR.

BY SAMUEL LOVER.

I.

OUTWARD BOUND.

BARNY O'REIRDON was a fisherman of Kinsale, and a heartier fellow never hauled a net nor cast a line into deep water: indeed Barny, independently of being a merry boy among his companions, a lover of good fun and good whiskey, was looked up to, rather, by his brother fishermen, as an intelligent fellow, and few boats brought more fish to market than Barny O'Reirdon's; his opinion on certain points in the craft was considered law, and in short, in his own little community, Barny was what is commonly called a leading man. Now your leading man is always jealous in an inverse ratio to the sphere of his influence, and the leader of a nation is less incensed at a rival's triumph than the great man of a village. If we pursue this descending scale, what a desperately jealous person the oracle of oyster-dredges and cockle-women must be! Such was Barny O'Reirdon.

Seated one night at a public house, the common resort of Barny and other marine curiosities, our hero got entangled in debate with what he called a strange sail, — that is to say, a man he had never met before, and whom he was inclined to treat rather magisterially upon nautical subjects; at the same time the stranger was equally inclined to assume the high hand over him, till at last the new-comer made a regular outbreak by exclaiming, "Ah, tare-and-ouns, lave aff your balderdash, Mr. O'Reirdon, by the powdhers o' war it's enough, so it is, to make a dog bate his father, to hear you goin' an as if you war Curlumberus or Sir Crustyphiz Wran, when ivery one knows the divil a farther you iver war nor ketchin crabs or drudgen oysters."

"Who towld you that, my Watherford Wondher?" rejoined Barny; "what the dickens do you know about sayfarin' farther nor fishin' for sprats in a bowl wid your grandmother?"

"O, baithershin," says the stranger.

"And who made you so bowld with my name?" demanded O'Reirdon.

"No matther for that," said the stranger; "but if you'd like for to know, shure it's your own cousin Molly Mullins knows me well, and maybe I don't know you and yours as well as the mother that bore you, aye, in throth; and sure I know the very thoughts o' you as well as if I was inside o' you, Barny O'Reirdon."

"By my sowl thin, you know betther thoughts than your own, Mr. Whippersnapper, if that's the name you go by."

"No, it's not the name I go by; I've as good a name

as your own, Mr. O'Reirdon, for want of a betther, and that's O'Sullivan."

"Throth there's more than there's good o' them," said Barny.

"Good or bad, I'm a cousin o' your own twice removed by the mother's side."

"And is it the Widda O'Sullivan's boy you'd be that left this come Candlemas four years?"

"The same."

"Throth thin you might know better manners to your eldhers, though I'm glad to see you, anyhow, agin; but a little thravellin' puts us beyant ourselves sometimes," said Barny, rather contemptuously.

"Throth I nivir bragged out o' myself yit, and it's what I say, that a man that's only fishin' aff the land all his life has no business to compare in the regard o' thracthericks wid a man that has sailed to Fingal."

This silenced any further argument on Barny's part. Where Fingal lay was all Greek to him; but, unwilling to admit his ignorance, he covered his retreat with the usual address of his countrymen, and turned the bitterness of debate into the cordial flow of congratulation at seeing his cousin again.

The liquor was frequently circulated, and the conversation began to take a different turn, in order to lead from that which had very nearly ended in a quarrel between O'Reirdon and his relation.

The state of the crops, county cess, road jobs, etc., became topics, and various strictures as to the utility of the latter were indulged in, while the merits of the neighboring farmers were canvassed.

1 *

"Why thin," said one, "that field o' whate o' Michael Coghlan is the finest field o' whate mortial eyes was ever set upon, — divil the likes iv it myself ever seen far or near."

"Throth thin sure enough," said another, "it promises to be a fine crap anyhow, and myself can't help thinkin' it quare that Mikee Coghlan, that's a plain-spoken, quite (quiet) man, and simple like, should have finer craps than Pether Kelly o' the big farm beyant, that knows all about the great saycrets o' the airth, and is knowledgeable to a degree, and has all the hard words that iver was coined at his fingers' ends."

"Faith, he has a power o' *blasthogue* about him sure enough," said the former speaker, " if that could do him any good, but he is n't fit to hould a candle to Michael Coghlan in the regard o' farmin'."

"Why blur and agers," rejoined the upholder of science, "sure he met the Scotch steward that the lord beyant has, one day, that I hear is a wondherful edicated man, and was brought over here to show us all a patthern, — well, Pether Kelly met him one day, and, by gor, he discoorsed him to a degree that the Scotch chap had n't a word left in his jaw."

"Well, and what was he the betther o' having more prate than a Scotchman?" asked the other.

"Why," answered Kelly's friend, "I think it stands to rayson that the man that done out the Scotch steward ought to know somethin' more about farmin' than Mikee Coghlan."

"Augh! don't talk to me about knowing," said the other, rather contemptuously. "Sure I gev in to you that he has a power o' prate, and the gift o' the gab, and all to that. I own to you that he has *the-o-ry*, and *che-mis-thery*, but he has n't the *craps*. Now, the man that has the craps is the man for my money."

"You're right, my boy," said O'Reirdon, with an approving thump of his brawny fist upon the table, "it's a little talk goes far, — *doin'* is the thing."

"Ah, yiz may run down larnin' if yiz like," said the undismayed stickler for theory versus practice, "but larnin' is a fine thing, and sure where would the world be at all only for it, sure where would the staymers (steamboats) be, only for larnin'?"

"Well," said O'Reirdon, "and the divil may care if we never seen them; I'd rather depind an wind and canvas any day than the likes o' them! What are they good for, but to turn good sailors into kitchen-maids, bilin' a big pot o' wather and oilin' their fire-irons, and throwin' coals an the fire? Augh? thim staymers is a disgrace to the say; they're for all the world like old fogies, smokin' from mornin' till night and doin' no good."

"Do you call it doin' no good to go fasther nor ships iver wint before?"

"Pooh; sure Solomon, queen o' Sheba, said there was time enough for all things."

"Thrue for you," said O'Sullivan, "*fair and aisy goes far in a day*, is a good ould sayin'."

"Well, maybe you'll own to the improvement they're makin' in the harbor o' Howth, beyant, in Dublin, is some good."

"We'll see whether it'll be an improvement first," said the obdurate O'Reirdon.

"Why, man alive, sure you'll own it's the greatest

o' good it is, takin' up the big rocks out o' the bottom o' the harbor."

"Well, an' where's the wondher o' that? sure we done the same here."

"O yis, but it was whin the tide was out and the rocks was bare; but up at Howth, they cut away the big rocks from undher the say intirely."

"O, be aisy; why how could they do that?"

"Aye, there's the matther, that's what larnin' can do; and wondherful it is intirely! and the way it is, is this, as I hear it, for I never seen it, but heerd it described by the lord to some gintlemin and ladies one day in his garden where I was helpin' the gardener to land some salary (celery). You see the ingineer goes down undher the wather intirely, and can stay there as long as he plazes."

"Whoo! and what o' that? Sure I heerd the long sailor say, that come from the Aystern Injees, that the ingineers there can a'most live under wather; and goes down looking for diamonds, and has a sledge-hammer in their hand, brakin' the diamonds when they're too big to take them up whole, all as one as men brakin' stones an the road."

"Well, I don't want to go beyant that; but the way the lord's ingineer goes down is, he has a little bell wid him, and while he has that little bell to ring, hurt nor harm can't come to him."

"Arrah be aisy."

"Divil a lie in it."

"Maybe it's a blissed bell," said O'Reirdon, crossing himself.

"No, it is not a blissed bell."

"Why thin now do you think me sich a born nathral as to give in to that? as if the ringin' iv the bell, barrin' it was a blissed bell, could do the like. I tell you it's unpossible."

"Ah, nothin' 's unpossible to God."

"Sure I was n't denyin' that; but I say the bell is unpossible."

"Why," said O'Sullivan, "you see he's not altogether complete in the demonstheration o' the mashine; it is not by the ringin' o' the bell it is done, but —"

"But what?" broke in O'Reirdon impatiently. "Do you mane for to say there is a bell in it at all at all?"

"Yis, I do," said O'Sullivan.

"I towld you so," said the promulgator of the story.

"Aye," said O'Sullivan, "but it is not by the ringin' iv the bell it is done."

"Well, how is it done then?" said the other, with a half-offended, half-supercilious air.

"It is done," said O'Sullivan, as he returned the look with interest, — "it is done entirely by jommethry."

"Oh! I understan' it now," said O'Reirdon, with an inimitable affectation of comprehension in the Oh! — "but to talk of the ringin' iv a bell doin' the like is beyant the beyants intirely, barrin', as I said before, it was a blissed bell, glory be to God!"

"And so you tell me, sir, it is jommethry," said the twice-discomfited man of science.

"Yis, sir," said O'Sullivan with an air of triumph, which rose in proportion as he carried the listeners along with him, — "jommethry."

"Well, have it your own way. There's them that won't hear rayson sometimes, nor have belief in larnin'; and you may say it's jommethry if you plaze; but I heerd them that knows betther than iver you knew say —"

"Whisht, whisht! and bad cess to you both," said O'Reirdon, "what the dickens are yiz goin' to fight about now, and sich good liquor before yiz? Hillo! there, Mrs. Quigley, bring uz another quart i' you plaze; aye, that's the chat, another quart. Augh! yiz may talk till yo're black in the face about your invintions, and your staymers, and bell ringin' and gash, and railroads; but here's long life and success to the man that invinted the impairil (imperial) quart; that was the rail beautiful invintion." And he took a long pull at the replenished vessel, which strongly indicated that the increase of its dimensions was a very agreeable *measure* to such as Barny.

After the introduction of this and *other* quarts, it would not be an easy matter to pursue the conversation that followed. Let us, therefore, transfer our story to the succeeding morning, when Barny O'Reirdon strolled forth from his cottage, rather later than usual, with his eyes bearing *eye* witness to the carouse of the preceding night. He had not a headache, however; whether it was that Barny was too experienced a campaigner under the banners of Bacchus, or that Mrs. Quigley's boast was a just one, namely, "that of all the drink in her house, there was'nt a headache in a hogshead of it," is hard to determine, but I rather incline to the strength of Barny's head.

Barny sauntered about in the sun, at which he often looked up, under the shelter of compressed bushy brows and long-lashed eyelids, and a shadowing hand across his forehead, to see "what o' day" it was; and, from the frequency of this action, it was evident the day was hanging heavily with Barny. He retired at last to a sunny nook in a neighboring field, and stretching himself at full length, basked in the sun, and began "to chew the cud of sweet and bitter thought." He first reflected on his own undoubted weight in his little community, but still he could not get over the annoyance of the preceding night, arising from his being silenced by O'Sullivan; "a chap," as he said himself, "that lift the place four years agon a brat iv a boy, and to think iv his comin' back and outdoin' his elders, that saw him runnin' about the place, a gassoon, that one could tache a few months before"; 't was too bad. Barny saw his reputation was in a ticklish position, and began to consider how his disgrace could be retrieved. The very name of Fingal was hateful to him; it was a plague-spot on his peace that festered there incurably. He first thought of leaving Kinsale altogether; but flight implied so much of defeat, that he did not long indulge in that notion. No; he *would* stay, "in spite of all the O'Sullivans, kith and kin, breed, seed, and generation." But at the same time he knew he should never hear the end of that hateful place, Fingal; and if Barny had had the power, he would have enacted a penal statute, making it death to name the accursed spot, wherever it was; but not being gifted with such legislative authority, he felt Kinsale was no place for him, if he would not submit to be flouted every hour out of the four-and-twenty, by man, woman, and child, that wished to annoy him. What was to be done? He was in the perplexing situation, to use his own words, "of the cat in the thripe shop," he did n't know which way to choose. At last, after turning himself over in the sun several times, a new idea struck him. Could n't he go to Fingal himself? and then he 'd be equal to that upstart, O'Sullivan. No sooner was the thought engendered, than Barny sprang to his feet a new man; his eye brightened, his step became once more elastic, — he walked erect, and felt himself to be all over Barny O'Reirdon once more. "Richard was himself again."

But where was Fingal? — there was the rub. That was a profound mystery to Barny, which, until discovered, must hold him in the vile bondage of inferiority. The plain-dealing reader would say, "Could n't he ask?" No, no; that would never do for Barny: that would be an open admission of ignorance his soul was above, and consequently Barny set his brains to work to devise measures of coming at the hidden knowledge by some circuitous route, that would not betray the end he was working for. To this purpose, fifty stratagems were raised, and demolished in half as many minutes, in the fertile brain of Barny, as he strided along the shore; and as he was working hard at the fifty-first, it was knocked all to pieces by his jostling against some one whom he never perceived he was approaching, so immersed was he in his speculations, and on looking up, who should it prove to be but his friend "the long sailor from the Aystern Injees." This was quite a godsend to Barny, and much beyond what he could have hoped for. Of all men under the sun, the long sailor was the man in a million for Barny's net at that minute, and accordingly he made a haul of him, and thought it the greatest catch he ever made in his life.

Barny and the long sailor were in close companionship for the remainder of the day, which was closed, as the preceding one, in a carouse; but on this occasion there was only a duet performance in honor of the jolly god, and the treat was at Barny's expense. What the nature of their conversation during the period was, I will not dilate on, but keep it as profound a secret as Barny himself did, and content myself with saying, that Barny looked a much happier man the next day. Instead of wearing his hat slouched, and casting his eyes on the ground, he walked about with his usual unconcern, and gave his nod and the passing word of *civilitude* to every friend he met; he rolled his quid of tobacco about in his jaw with an air of superior enjoyment, and if disturbed in his narcotic amusement by a question, he took his own time to eject "the leperous distilment" before he answered the querist, — a happy composure, that bespoke a man quite at ease with himself. It was in this agreeable spirit that Barny bent his course to the house of Peter Kelly, the owner of the "big farm beyant," before alluded to, in order to put in practice a plan he had formed for the fulfilment of his determination of rivalling O'Sullivan.

He thought it probable that Peter Kelly, being one of the "snuggest" men in the neighborhood, would be a likely person to join him in a "spec," as he called it (a favorite abbreviation of his for the word "speculation"), and accordingly, when he reached the "big-farm house," he accosted the owner with his usual "God save you."

"God save you kindly, Barny," returned Peter Kelly; "an' what is it brings you here, Barny," asked Peter, "this fine day, instead o' being out in the boat?"

"O, I'll be out in the boat soon enough, and it's far enough too I'll be in her; an' indeed it's partly that same is bringin' me here to yourself."

"Why, do you want me to go along wid you, Barny?"

"Troth an' I don't, Mr. Kelly. You're a knowledgeable man an land, but I'm afeared it's a bad bargain you'd be at say."

"And what wor you talking about me and your boat for?"

"Why, you see, sir, it was in the regard of a little bit o' business, an' if you'd come wid me and take a turn in the praty-field, I'll be behouldin' to you, and maybe you'll hear somethin' that won't be displazin' to you."

"An' welkim, Barny," said Peter Kelly.

When Barny and Peter were in the "praty-field," Barny opened the trenches (I don't mean the potato trenches), but, in military parlance, he opened the trenches and laid siege to Peter Kelly, setting forth the extensive profits that had been realized at various "specs" that had been made by his neighbors in exporting potatoes. "And sure," said Barny, "why shouldn't *you* do the same, and they are ready to your hand? as much as to say, *why don't you profit by me, Peter Kelly?* And the boat is below there in the harbor, and, I'll say this much, the divil a betther boat is betune this and herself."

"Indeed, I b'lieve so, Barny," said Peter, "for considhering where we stand, at this present, there's no boat at all at all betune us." And Peter laughed with infinite pleasure at his own hit.

"O, well, you know what I mane, anyhow, an', as I said before, the boat is a darlint boat, and as for him that commands her — I b'lieve I need say nothin' about that." And Barny gave a toss of his head and a sweep of his open hand, more than doubling the laudatory nature of his comment on himself.

But, as the Irish saying is, "to make a long story short," Barny prevailed on Peter Kelly to make an export; but in the nature of the venture they did not agree. Barny had proposed potatoes; Peter said there were enough of them already where he was going; and Barny rejoined that, "praties were so good in themselves there never could be too much o' thim anywhere." But Peter being a knowledgeable man, and up to all the "saycrets o' the airth, and understanding the the-o-ry and the che-mis-thery," overruled Barny's proposition, and determined upon a cargo of *scalpeens* (which name they gave to pickled mackerel), as a preferable merchandise, quite forgetting that Dublin Bay herrings were a much better and as cheap a commodity, at the command of the Fingalians. But in many similar mistakes the ingenious Mr. Kelly has been paralleled by other speculators. But that is neither here nor there, and it was all one to Barny whether his boat was freighted with potatoes or *sculpeens*, so long as he had the honor and glory of becoming a navigator, and being as good as O'Sullivan.

Accordingly the boat was laden and all got in readiness for putting to sea, and nothing was now wanting but Barny's orders to haul up the gaff and shake out the jib of his hooker.

But this order Barny refrained to give, and for the first time in his life exhibited a disinclination to leave the shore. One of his fellow-boatmen, at last, said to him, "Why thin, Barny O'Reirdon, what the divil is come over you, at all at all? What's the maynin' of your loitherin' about here, and the boat ready and a lovely fine breeze aff o' the land?"

"O, never you mind; I b'lieve I know my own business anyhow, an' it's hard, so it is, if a man can't ordher his own boat to sail when he plazes."

"O, I was only thinking it quare; and a pity more betoken, as I said before, to lose the beautiful breeze, and —"

"Well, just keep your thoughts to yourself, i' you plaze, and stay in the boat as I bid you, and don't be out of her on your apperl, by no manner o' manes, for one minit, for you see I don't know when it may be plazin' to me to go aboord an' set sail."

"Well, all I can say is, I never seen you afeared to go to say before."

"Who says I'm afeared?" said O'Reirdon; "you'd betther not say that agin, or in troth I'll give you a leatherin' that won't be for the good o' your health, —

troth, for three straws this minit I 'd lave you that your own mother would n't know you with the lickin' I 'd give you; but I scorn your dirty insinuation; no man ever seen Barny O'Reirdon afeard yet, anyhow. Howld your prate, I tell you, and look up to your betthers. What do you know iv navigation? Maybe you think it's as aisy for to sail on a voyage as to go start a fishin'." And Barny turned on his heel and left the shore.

The next day passed without the hooker sailing, and Barny gave a most sufficient reason for the delay, by declaring that he had a warnin' givin him in a dhrame (Glory be to God), and that it was given to him to understand (under Heaven) that it would n't be lucky that day.

Well, the next day was Friday, and Barny, of course, would not sail any more than any other sailor who could help it on this unpropitious day. On Saturday, however, he came, running in a great hurry down to the shore, and, jumping aboard, he gave orders to make all sail, and taking the helm of the hooker, he turned her head to the sea, and soon the boat was cleaving the blue waters with a velocity seldom witnessed in so small a craft, and scarcely conceivable to those who have not seen the speed of a Kinsale hooker.

"Why, thin, you tuk the notion mighty suddint, Barny," said the fisherman next in authority to O'Reirdon, as soon as the bustle of getting the boat under way had subsided.

"Well, I hope it's plazin' to you at last," said Barny, "troth one ud think you were never at say before, you wor in such a hurry to be off; as new-fangled a'most as the child with a play toy."

"Well," said the other of Barny's companions, for there were but two with him in the boat, "I was thinkin' myself, as well as Jemmy, that we lost two fine days for nothin', and we'd be there a'most, maybe, now, if we sail'd three days agon."

"Don't b'lieve it," said Barny, emphatically. "Now, don't you know yourself that there is some days that the fish won't come near the lines at all, and that we might as well be castin' our nets on the dhry land as in the say, for all we'll catch if we start on an unlooky day; and sure, I towld you I was waitin' only till I had it given to me to undherstan' that it was looky to sail, and I go bail we'll be there sooner than if we started three days agon, for if you don't start with good look before you, faix maybe it's never at all to the end o' your trip you'll come."

"Well, there's no use in talkin' aboot it now, anyhow; but when do you expec' to be there?"

"Why, you see we must wait antil I can tell how the wind is like to hould on, before I can make up my mind to that."

"But you're sure now, Barny, that you're up to the coorse you have to run?"

"See now, lave me alone and don't be cross crassquestionin' me — tare-an-ouns, do you think me sich a bladdherang as for to go to shuperinscribe a thing I was n't aiquil to?"

"No; I was only goin' to ax you what coorse you wor goin' to steer?"

"You'll find out soon enough when we get there — and so I bid you agin lay me alone, — just keep your toe in your pump. Shure I'm here at the helm, and a weight on my mind, and it's fitther for you, Jim, to mind your own business and lay me to mind mine; away wid you there and be handy, haul taut that foresheet there, we must run close on the wind; be handy, boys; make everything dhraw."

These orders were obeyed, and the hooker soon passed to windward of a ship that left the harbor before her, but could not hold on a wind with the same tenacity as the hooker, whose qualities in this particular render it peculiarly suitable for the purposes to which it is applied, namely, pilot and fishing boats.

We have said a ship left the harbor before the hooker had set sail; and it is now fitting to inform the reader that Barny had contrived, in the course of his last meeting with the "long sailor," to ascertain that this ship, then lying in the harbor, was going to the very place Barny wanted to reach. Barny's plan of action was decided upon in a moment; he had now nothing to do but to watch the sailing of the ship and follow in her course. Here was, at once, a new mode of navigation discovered.

The stars, twinkling in mysterious brightness through the silent gloom of night, were the first encouraging, because visible, guides to the adventurous mariners of antiquity. Since then, the sailor, encouraged by a bolder science, relies on the unseen agency of nature, depending on the fidelity of an atom of iron to the mystic law that claims its homage in the north. This is one refinement of science upon another. But the beautiful simplicity of Barny O'Reirdon's philosophy cannot be too much admired, — to follow the ship that is going to the same place. Is not this navigation made easy?

But Barny, like many a great man before him, seemed not to be aware of how much credit he was entitled to for his invention, for he did not divulge to his companions the originality of his proceeding; he wished them to believe he was only proceeding in the commonplace manner, and had no ambition to be distinguished as the happy projector of so simple a practice.

For this purpose he went to windward of the ship and then fell off again, allowing her to pass him, as he did not wish even those on board the ship to suppose he was following in their wake; for Barny, like all people that are quite full of one scheme, and fancy everybody is watching them, dreaded lest any one should fathom his motives. All that day Barny held on the same course as his leader, keeping at a respectful distance, however, "for fear 't would look like dodging her," as he said to himself; but as night closed in, so closed in Barny with the ship, and kept a sharp lookout that she should not give him the slip. The next morning dawned, and found the hooker and ship companions still; and thus matters proceeded for four days, during which entire time they had not seen land since their first losing sight of it, although the weather was clear.

"By my sowl," thought Barny, "the channel must be mighty wide in these parts, and for the last day or so we 've been goin' purty free with a flowing sheet, and I wondher we are n't closin' in wid the shore by this time; or maybe it's farther off than I thought it was." His companions, too, began to question Barny on the subject, but to their queries he presented an impenetrable front of composure, and said "it was always the best plan to keep a good bowld offin'." In two days more, however, the weather began to be sensibly warmer, and Barny and his companions remarked that it was "goin' to be the finest saysou — God bless it — that ever kem out o' the skies for many a long year, and maybe it 's the whate would not be beautiful, and a great dale of it."

It was at the end of a week that the ship which Barny had hitherto kept ahead of him showed symptoms of bearing down upon him, as he thought, and, sure enough, she did; and Barny began to conjecture what the deuce the ship could want with him, and commenced inventing answers to the questions he thought it possible might be put to him in case the ship spoke him. He was soon put out of suspense by being hailed and ordered to run under her lee, and the captain, looking over the quarter, asked Barny where he was going.

"Faith then, I'm goin' an my business," said Barny.

"But where?" said the captain.

"Why, sure, an' it's no matther where a poor man like me id be goin'," said Barny.

"Only I'm curious to know what the deuce you've been following my ship for, the last week."

"Follyin' your ship! Why, thin, blur-an-agers, do you think it's follyin' yiz I am?"

"It's very like it," said the captain.

"Why, did two people niver thravel the same road before?"

"I don't say they did n't; but there's a great difference between a ship of seven hundred tons and a hooker."

"O, as for that matther," said Barny, "the same high-road sarves a coach and four and a lowback car, the thravellin' tinker an' a lord a' horseback."

"That's very true," said the captain, "but the cases are not the same, Paddy, and I can't conceive what the devil brings *you* here."

"And who ax'd you to consayve anything about it?" asked Barny, somewhat sturdily.

"D—n me, if I can imagine what you 're about, my fine fellow," said the captain; "and my own notion is, that you don't know where the d—l you 're going yourself."

"O *baithershin!*" said Barny, with a laugh of derision.

"Why then do you object to tell?" said the captain.

"Arrah sure, captain, an' don't you know that sometimes vessels is bound to sail under *saycret ordhers?*" said Barny, endeavoring to foil the question by badinage.

There was a universal laugh from the deck of the ship, at the idea of a fishing-boat sailing under secret orders; for, by this time, the whole broadside of the vessel was crowded with grinning mouths and wondering eyes at Barny and his boat.

"O, it's a thrifle makes fools laugh," said Barny.

"Take care, my fine fellow, that you don't be laughing at the wrong side of your mouth before long, for

I've a notion that you're cursedly in the wrong box, as cunning a fellow as you think yourself. D—n your stupid head, can't you tell what brings you here?"

"Why, thin, by gor, one id think the whole say belonged to you, you're so mighty bowld in axin' questions an it. Why, tare-an-ouns, sure I've as much right to be here as you, though I have n't as big a ship nor as fine a coat, — but maybe I can take as good a sailin' out o' the one, and has as bowld a heart under th' other."

"Very well," said the captain, "I see there's no use in talking to you, so go to the d—l your own way." And away bore the ship, leaving Barny in indignation and his companions in wonder.

"An' why would n't you tell him?" said they to Barny.

"Why, don't you see," said Barny, whose object was now to blind them, — "don't you see, how do I know but maybe he might be goin' to the same place himself, and maybe he has a cargo of *scalpeens* as well as uz, and wants to get before us there."

"True for you, Barny," said they. "By dad, you're right." And their inquiries being satisfied, the day passed as former ones had done, in pursuing the course of the ship.

In four days more, however, the provisions in the hooker began to fail, and they were obliged to have recourse to the *scalpeens* for sustenance, and Barny then got seriously uneasy at the length of the voyage, and the likely greater length, for anything he could see to the contrary; and, urged at last by his own alarms and those of his companions, he was enabled, as the wind was light, to gain on the ship, and when he found himself alongside he demanded a parley with the captain.

The captain, on hearing that the "hardy hooker," as she got christened, was under his lee, came on deck; and as soon as he appeared Barny cried out, —

"Why, thin, blur-an-agers, Captain dear, do you expec' to be there soon?"

"Where?" said the captain.

"O, you know yourself!" said Barny.

"It's well for me I do," said the captain.

"Thrue for you, indeed, your honor," said Barny, in his most insinuating tone; "but whin will you be at the ind o' your voyage, Captain jewel?"

"I daresay in about three months," said the captain.

"O Holy Mother!" ejaculated Barny; "three months! — arrah, it's jokin' you are, Captain dear, and only want to freken me."

"How should I frighten you?" asked the captain.

"Why, thin, your honor, to tell God's thruth, I heard you were goin' *there*, an' as I wanted to go there too, I thought I couldn't do better nor to folly a knowledgeable gintleman like yourself, and save myself the throuble iv findin' it out."

"And where do you think I *am* going?" said the captain.

"Why, thin," said Barny, "isn't it to Fingal?"

"No," said the captain, "it's to *Bengal*."

"O Gog's blakey!" said Barny, "what'll I do now, at all at all?"

II.

HOMEWARD BOUND.

The captain ordered Barny on deck, as he wished to have some conversation with him on what he, very naturally, considered a most extraordinary adventure. Heaven help the captain! he knew little of Irishmen, or he would not have been so astonished. Barny made his appearance. Puzzling question and more puzzling answer followed in quick succession between the commander and Barny, who, in the midst of his dilemma, stamped about, thumped his head, squeezed his caubeen into all manner of shapes, and vented his despair anathematically: "O, my heavy hathred to you, you tarnal thief iv a long sailor, it's a purty scrape yiv led me into. By gor, I thought it was *Fingal* he said, and now I hear it is *Bingal*. O, the divil sweep you for navigation, why did I meddle or make wid you at all at all? And my curse light on you, Terry O'Sullivan, why did I iver come across you, you onlooky vagabone, to put sich thoughts in my head? And so it's *Bingal*, and not *Fingal*, you're goin' to, Captain?"

"Yes, indeed, Paddy."

"An' might I be so bowld to ax, Captain, is Bingal much farther nor Fingal?"

"A trifle or so, Paddy?"

"Och, thin, millia murther, weirasthru, how'll I iver get there at all at all?" roared out poor Barny.

"By turning about, and getting back the road you've come, as fast as you can."

"Is it back? O Queen iv Heaven! an' how will I iver get back?" said the bewildered Barny.

"Then, you don't know your course, it appears?"

"O, faix I knew it iligant, as long as your honor was before me."

"But you don't know your course back?"

"Why, indeed, not to say rightly all out, your honor."

"Can't you steer?" said the captain.

"The divil a betther hand at the tiller in all Kinsale," said Barny, with his usual brag.

"Well, so far so good," said the captain. "And you know the points of the compass, — you have a compass, I suppose?"

"A compass! by my sowl an' it's not let alone a compass, but a *pair* a compasses I have, that my brother the carpinthir left me for a keepsake whin he wint abroad; but, indeed, as for the points o' thim I can't say much, for the childer spylt thim intirely, rootin' holes in the flure."

"What the plague are you talking about?" asked the captain.

"Was n't your honor discoorsin' me about the points o' the compasses?"

"Confound your thick head!" said the captain. "Why, what an ignoramus you must be, not to know what a compass is, and you at sea all your life? Do you even know the cardinal points?"

"The cardinals! faix, an' it's a great respect I have for them, your honor. Sure, ar' n't they belongin' to the pope?"

"Confound you, you blockhead!" roared the captain, in a rage, — "'t would take the patience of the pope and the cardinals, and the cardinal virtues into the bargain, to keep one's temper with you. Do you know the four points of the wind?"

"By my sowl, I do, and more."

"Well, never mind more, but let us stick to four. You 're sure you know the four points of the wind?"

"By dad, it would be a quare thing if a seyfarin' man did n't know somethin' about the wind anyhow. Why, Captain dear, you must take me for a nathral intirely, to suspect me o' the like o' not knowin' all about the wind. By gor, I know as much o' the wind a'most as a pig."

"Indeed, I believe so," laughed out the captain.

"O, you may laugh if you plaze, and I see by the same that you don't know about the pig, with all your edication, Captain."

"Well, what about the pig?"

"Why, sir, did you never hear a pig can see the wind?"

"I can't say that I did."

"O, thin he does, and for that rayson who has a right to know more about it?"

"You don't, for one, I dare say, Paddy; and maybe you have a pig aboard to give you information."

"Sorra taste, your honor, not as much as a rasher o' bacon; but it's maybe your honor never seen a pig tossing up his snout, consaited like, and running like mad afore a storm."

"Well, what if I have?"

"Well, sir, that is when they see the wind a-comin'."

"Maybe so, Paddy, but all this knowledge in piggery

won't find you your way home; and, if you take my advice, you will give up all thoughts of endeavoring to find your way back, and come on board. You and your messmates, I dare say, will be useful hands, with some teaching; but, at all events, I cannot leave you here on the open sea, with every chance of being lost."

"Why, thin, indeed, and I'm behowlden to your honor; and it's the hoighth o' kindness, so it is, you offer; and it's nothin' else but a gintleman you are, every inch o' you; but I hope it's not so bad wid us yet, as to do the likes o' that."

"I think it's bad enough," said the captain, "when you are without a compass and knowing nothing of your course, and nearly a hundred and eighty leagues from land."

"An' how many miles would that be, Captain?"

"Three times as many."

"I never larned the rule o' three, Captain, and maybe your honor id tell me yourself."

"That is rather more than five hundred miles."

"Five hundred miles!" shouted Barny. "O, the Lord look down upon us! how'll we ever get back?"

"That's what I say," said the captain; "and therefore, I recommend you to come aboard with me."

"And where 'ud the hooker be all the time?" said Barny.

"Let her go adrift," was the answer.

"Is it the darlint boat? O, by dad, I'll never hear o' that at all."

"Well, then, stay in her and be lost. Decide upon the matter at once, either come on board or cast off."

And the captain was turning away as he spoke, when Barny called after him, "Arrah, thin, your honor, don't go jist for one minit antil I ax you one word more. If I wint wid you, whin would I be home again?"

"In about seven months."

"O, thin, that puts the wig an it at wanst. I dar'n't go at all."

"Why, seven months are not long passing."

"Thrue for you, in throth," said Barny, with a shrug of his shoulders. "Faix, it's myself knows, to my sorrow, the half year comes round mighty suddint, and the lord's agint comes for the thrifle o' rent."

"Then what's your objection, as to the time?" asked the captain.

"Arrah, sure, sir, what would the woman that owns me do while I was away? and maybe it's break her heart the craythur would, thinking I was lost intirely; and who'd be at home to take care o' the childher' and airn thim the bit and the sup, whin I'd be away? and who knows but it's all dead they'd be afore I got back? Och hone! sure the heart id fairly break in my body, if hurt or harm kem to them, through me. So, say no more, Captain dear, only give me a thrifle o' directions how I'm to make an offer at gettin' home, and it's myself that will pray for you night, noon, and mornin' for that same."

"Well, Paddy," said the captain, "as you are determined to go back, in spite of all I can say, you must attend to me well while I give you as simple instructions as I can. You say you know the four points of the wind, north, south, east, and west."

"Yes, sir."

"How do you know them? for I must see that you are not likely to make a mistake. How do you know the points?"

"Why, you see, sir, the sun, God bless it, rises in the aist, and sets in the west, which stands to raison; and whin you stand bechuxt the aist and the west, the north is forninst you."

"And when the north is fornenst you, as you say, is the east on your right or your left hand?"

"On the right hand, your honor."

"Well, I see you know that much, however. Now," said the captain, "the moment you leave the ship, you must steer a northeast course, and you will make some land near home in about a week, if the wind holds as it is now, and it is likely to do so; but, mind me, if you turn out of your course in the smallest degree you are a lost man."

"Many thanks to your honor!"

"And how are you off for provisions?"

"Why, thin, indeed, in the regard o' that same we are in the hoighth o' distress, for exceptin' the scalpeens, sorra taste passed our lips for these four days."

"O, you poor devils!" said the commander, in a tone of sincere commiseration, "I'll order you some provisions on board before you start."

"Long life to your honor! and I'd like to drink the health of so noble a gintleman."

"I understand you, Paddy, you shall have grog too."

"Musha, the heavens shower blessin's an you, I pray

the Virgin Mary and the twelve apostles, Matthew, Mark, Luke, and John, not forgettin' Saint Pathrick."

"Thank you, Paddy; but keep your prayers for yourself, for you need them all to help you home again."

"Oh! never fear, when the thing is to be done, I'll do it, by dad, wid a heart and a half. Aud sure, your honor, God is good, an' will mind dessolute craythurs like uz on the wild oceant as well as ashore."

While some of the ship's crew were putting the captain's benevolent intentions to Barny and his companions into practice, by transferring some provisions to the hooker, the commander entertained himself by further conversation with Barny, who was the greatest original he had ever met. In the course of their colloquy, Barny drove many hard queries at the captain, respecting the wonders of the nautical profession, and at last put the question to him plump:—

"Oh! thin, Captain dear, and how is it at all at all, that you make your way over the wide says intirely to them furrin parts?"

"You would not understand, Paddy, if I attempted to explain to you."

"Sure enough, indeed, your honor, and I ask your pardon, only I was curious to know, and sure no wondher."

"It requires various branches of knowledge to make a navigator."

"Branches," said Barny, "by gar I think it id take the whole tree o' knowledge to make it out. And that place you are going to, sir, that *Bi*n*gal* (oh! bad luck to it for a *Bin*gal, it's the sore *Bin*gal to me), is it so far off as you say?"

"Yes, Paddy, half round the world."

"Is it round in airnest, Captain dear? Round about!"

"Aye, indeed."

"O, thin, ar' n't you afeard that whin you come to the top and that you're obleedged to go down, that you'd go slidderhin away intirely, and never be able to stop, maybe. It's bad enough, so it is, going down hill by land, but it must be the dickens all out by wather."

"But there is no hill, Paddy; don't you know that water is always level?"

"By dad, it's very *flat* anyhow, and by the same token it's seldom I throuble it; but sure, your honor, if the wather is level, how do you make out that it is *round* you go?"

"That is a part of the knowledge I was speaking to you about," said the captain.

"Musha, bad luck to you, knowledge, but you're a quare thing! — and where is it Bingal, bad cess to it, would be at all at all?"

"In the East Indies."

"O, that is where they make the *tay*, is n't it, sir?"

"No, where the tea grows is further still."

"Further! why that must be the ind of the world intirely; and they don't make it, thin, sir, but it grows, you tell me."

"Yes, Paddy."

"Is it like hay, your honor?"

"Not exactly, Paddy; what puts hay in your head?"

"Oh! only bekase I hear them call it Bo*hay*."

"A most logical deduction, Paddy."

"And is it a great deal farther, your honor, the *tay* country is?"

"Yes, Paddy, China it is called."

"That's, I suppose, what we call Chaynce, sir?"

"Exactly, Paddy."

"By dad, I never could come at it rightly before, why it was nathral to drink tay out o' chaynee. I ax your honor's pardon for bein' troublesome, but I hard tell from the long sailor, iv a place they call Japan, in them furrin parts, and *is* it there, your honor?"

"Quite true, Paddy."

"And I suppose it's there the blackin' comes from."

"No, Paddy, you are out there."

"O well, I thought it stood to rayson, as I heerd of Japan blackin', sir, that it would be there it kem from; besides, — as the blacks themselves, — the naygers, I mane, is in them parts."

"The negroes are in Africa, Paddy, much nearer to us."

"God betune us and harm. I hope I would not be too near them," said Barny.

"Why, what's your objection?"

"Arrah sure, sir, they're hardly mortials at all, but has the mark o' the bastes an thim."

"How do you make out that, Paddy?"

"Why sure, sir, and didn't Natur make thim wid wool on their heads, plainly makin' it undherstood to Chrishthans, that they were little more nor cattle?"

"I think your head is a wool-gathering now, Paddy," said the captain, laughing.

"Faix, maybe so, indeed," answered Barny, good-humoredly, "but it's seldom I ever went out to look for wool and kem home shorn, anyhow," said he, with a look of triumph.

"Well, you won't have that to say for the future, Paddy," said the captain, laughing again.

"My name's not Paddy, your honor," said Barny, returning the laugh, but seizing the opportunity to turn the joke aside, that was going against him; "my name is n't Paddy, sir, but Barny."

"O, if it was Solomon, you'll be bare enough when you go home this time; you have not gathered much this trip, Barny."

"Sure, I've been gathering knowledge, anyhow, your honor," said Barny, with a significant look at the captain, and a complimentary tip of his hand to his caubeen, "and God bless you for being so good to me."

"And what's your name besides Barny?" asked the captain.

"O'Reirdon, your honor, — Barny O'Reirdon's my name."

"Well, Barny O'Reirdon, I won't forget your name nor yourself in a hurry, for you are certainly the most original navigator I ever had the honor of being acquainted with."

"Well," said Barny, with a triumphant toss of his head, "I have done Terry O'Sullivan, at any rate, the devil a half so far he ever was, and that's a comfort. I have muzzled his clack for the rest iv his life, and he won't be comin' over us wid the pride iv his *Fingal* while I'm to the fore, that was a'most at *Bingal*!"

"Terry O'Sullivan, — who is he, pray?" said the captain.

"O, he's a scut iv a chap that's not worth your axin' for, — he's not worth your honor's notice, — a braggin' poor craythur. O, wait till I get home, and the devil a more braggin' they'll hear out of his jaw."

"Indeed then, Barny, the sooner you turn your face toward home the better," said the captain: "since you will go, there is no need of your losing more time."

"Thrue for you, your honor, — and sure it's well for me I had the luck to meet with the likes o' your honor, that explained the ins and the outs iv it, to me, and laid it all down as plain as prent."

"Are you sure you remember my directions?" said the captain.

"Troth an I'll niver forget them to the day o' my death, and is bound to pray, more betoken, for you and yours."

"Don't mind praying for me till you get home, Barny; but answer me, how are you to steer when you shall leave me?"

"The nor-aist coorse, your honor, that's the coorse agin the world."

"Remember that! Never alter that course till you see land, — let nothing make you turn out of a northeast course."

"Throth an' that would be the dirty turn, seein' that it was yourself that ordhered it. O no, I'll depend my life an the *nor-aist coorse*, and God help any that comes betune me an' it, — I'd run him down if he was my father."

"Well, good by, Barny."

"Good by, and God bless you, your honor, and send you safe."

"That's a wish you want for yourself, Barny, — never fear for me, but mind yourself well."

"O, sure, I'm as good as at home wanst I know the way, barrin' the wind is conthrary; sure the nor-aist coorse 'll do the business complate. Good by, your honor, and long life to you, and more power to your elbow, and a light heart and a heavy purse to you evermore, I pray the blessed Virgin and all the saints, amin!" And so saying, Barny descended the ship's side, and once more assumed the helm of the "hardy hooker."

The two vessels now separated on their opposite courses. What a contrast their relative situations afforded! Proudly the ship bore away under her lofty and spreading canvas, cleaving the billows before her, manned by an able crew, and under the guidance of experienced officers; the finger of science to point the course of her progress, the faithful chart to warn of the hidden rock and the shoal, the long line and the quadrant to measure her march and prove her position. The poor little hooker cleft not the billows, each wave lifted her on its crest like a sea-bird; but the three inexperienced fishermen to manage her; no certain means to guide them over the vast ocean they had to traverse, and the holding of the "fickle wind" the only *chance* of their escape from perishing in the wilderness of waters. By the one, the feeling excited is supremely that of man's power. By the other, of his utter helplessness.

To the one, the expanse of ocean could scarcely be considered "trackless." To the other, it was a waste indeed.

Yet the cheer that burst from the ship, at parting, was answered as gayly from the hooker as though the odds had not been so fearfully against her, and no blither heart beat on board the ship than that of Barny O'Reirdon.

Happy light-heartedness of my countrymen! How kindly have they been fortified by nature against the assaults of adversity; and if they blindly rush into dangers, they cannot be denied the possession of gallant hearts to fight their way out of them.

But each hurrah became less audible; by degrees the cheers dwindled into faintness, and finally were lost in the eddies of the breeze.

The first feeling of loneliness that poor Barny experienced was when he could no longer hear the exhilarating sound. The plash of the surge, as it broke on the bows of his little boat, was uninterrupted by the kindred sound of human voice; and, as it fell upon his ear, it smote upon his heart. But he replied, waved his hat, and the silent signal was answered from those on board the ship.

"Well, Barny," said Jemmy, "what was the captain sayin' to you at the time you wor wid him?"

"Lay me alone," said Barny, "I'll talk to you when I see her out o' sight, but not a word till thin. I'll look afther him, the rale gintleman that he is, while there's a topsail of his ship to be seen, and then I'll send my blessin' afther him, and pray for his good fortune wherever he goes, for he's the right sort and nothin' else." And Barny kept his word, and when his straining eye could no longer trace a line of the ship, the captain certainly had the benefit of "a poor man's blessing."

The sense of utter loneliness and desolation had not come upon Barny until now; but he put his trust in the goodness of Providence, and in a fervent mental outpouring of prayer resigned himself to the care of his Creator. With an admirable fortitude, too, he assumed a composure to his companions that was a stranger to his heart; and we all know how the burden of anxiety is increased when we have none with whom to sympathize. And this was not all. He had to affect ease and confidence, for Barny not only had no dependence on the firmness of his companions to go through the undertaking before them, but dreaded to betray to them how he had imposed on them in the affair. Barny was equal to all this. He had a stout heart, and was an admirable actor; yet, for the first hour after the ship was out of sight, he could not quite recover himself, and every now and then, unconsciously, he would look back with a wishful eye to the point where last he saw her. Poor Barny had lost his leader.

The night fell, and Barny stuck to the helm as long as nature could sustain want of rest, and then left it in charge of one of his companions, with particular directions how to steer, and ordered, if any change in the wind occurred, that they should instantly awake him. He could not sleep long, however; the fever of anxiety was upon him, and the morning had not long dawned when he awoke. He had not well rubbed his eyes and looked about him, when he thought he saw a ship in the distance approaching them. As the haze cleared away, she showed distinctly bearing down toward the hooker. On board the ship, the hooker, in such a sea, caused surprise as before, and in about an hour she was so close as to hail, and order the hooker to run under her lee.

"The devil a taste," said Barny. "I'll not quit my *nor-aist coorse* for the king of Ingland, nor Bonyparty into the bargain. Bad cess to you, do you think I've nothin' to do but plaze you?"

Again he was hailed.

"Oh! bad luck to the toe I'll go to you."

Another hail.

"Spake loudher you'd betther," said Barny, jeeringly, still holding on his course.

A gun was fired ahead of him.

"By my sowl you spoke loudher that time, sure enough," said Barny.

"Take care, Barny," cried Jemmy and Peter together. "Blur-an-agers, man, we'll be kilt if you don't go to them."

"Well, and we'll be lost if we turn out iv our *nor-aist coorse*, and that's as broad as it's long. Let them hit iz if they like; sure it ud be a pleasanter death nor starvin' at say. I tell you agin I'll turn out o' my *nor-aist coorse* for no man."

A shotted gun was fired. The shot hopped on the water as it passed before the hooker.

"Phew! you missed it, like your mammy's blessin'," said Barny.

"O murther!" said Jemmy, "did n't you see the ball hop aff the wather forninst you. O murther, what 'ud we ha' done if we wor there at all at all?"

"Why, we 'd have taken the ball at the hop," said Barny, laughing, "accordin' to the ould sayin'."

Another shot was ineffectually fired.

"I 'm thinking that 's a Connaughtman that 's shootin'," said Barny, with a sneer.* The allusion was so relished by Jemmy and Peter, that it excited a smile in the midst of their fears from the cannonade.

Again the report of the gun was followed by no damage.

"Augh! never heed them!" said Barny, contemptuously. "'It 's a barkin' dog that never bites,' as the owld sayin' says." And the hooker was soon out of reach of further annoyance.

"Now, what a pity it was, to be sure," said Barny, "that I would n't go aboord to plaze them. Now who 's right? Ah, lave me alone always, Jimmy; did you iver know me wrong yet?"

"O, you may hillow now that you are out o' the wood, said Jemmy, "but, accordin' to my idays, it was runnin' a grate risk to be conthrary wid them at all, and they shootin' balls afther us."

"Well, what matther?" said Barny, "since they wor only blind gunners, *an' I knew it;* besides, as I said afore, I won't turn out o' my *nor-aist coorse* for no man."

---

* This is an allusion of Barny's to a prevalent saying in Ireland, addressed to a sportsman who returns home unsuccessful, "So you 've killed what the Connaughtman shot at."

"That's a new turn you tuk lately," said Peter. "What's the raison you're runnin' a nor-aist coorse now, an' we never hear'd iv it afore at all, till afther you quitted the big ship?"

"Why, thin, are you sich an ignoramus all out," said Barny, "as not for to know that in navigation you must lie an a great many different tacks before you can make the port you steer for?"

"Only I think," said Jemmy, "that it's back intirely we're goin' now, and I can't make out the rights o' that at all."

"Why," said Barny, who saw the necessity of mystifying his companions a little, "you see, the captain towld me that I kum around, an' rekimminded me to go th' other way."

"Faix, it's the first time I ever heard o' goin' round by say," said Jemmy.

"Arrah, sure, that's part o' the sayerets o' navigation, and the varrious branches o' knowledge that is requizit for a navigator; and that's what the captain, God bless him, and myself was discoorsin' an aboord; and, like a rale gintleman as he is, Barny, says he; Sir, says I; you've come the round, says he. I know that, says I, bekase I like to keep a good bowld offin', says I, in contrairy places. Spoke like a good sayman, says he. That's my principles, says I. They're the right sort, says he. But, says he (no offence), I think you wor wrong, says he, to pass the short turn in the ladieshoes,* says he. I know, says I, you mane beside the

---

* Some offer Barny is making at latitudes.

three-spike headlan'. That's the spot, says he, I see you know it. As well as I know my father, says I."

"Why, Barny," said Jemmy, interrupting him, "we seen no headlan' at all."

"Whisht, whisht!" said Barny, "bad cess to you, don't thwart me. We passed it in the night, and you could n't see it. Well, as I was saying, I knew it as well as I know my father, says I, but I gev the preference to go the round, says I. You 're a good sayman for that same, says he, an' it would be right at any other time than this present, says he, but it's onpossible now, tee-totally, on account o' the war, says he. Tare alive, says I, what war? An' did n't you hear o' the war? says he. Divil a word, says I. Why, says he, the naygers has made war on the king o' Chaynee, says he, bekase he refused them any more tay; an' with that, what did they do, says he, but they put a lumbargo on all the vessels that sails the round, an' that's the rayson, says he, I carry guns, as you may see; and I rekimmind you, says he, to go back, for you 're not able for thim, and that's jist the way iv it. An' now, was n't it looky that I kem acrass him at all, or maybe we might be cotch by the naygers, and ate up alive."

"O, thin, indeed, and that's thrue," said Jemmy and Peter, "and whin will we come to the short turn?"

"O, never mind," said Barny, "you'll see it when you get there; but wait till I tell you more about the captain, and the big ship. He said, you know, that he carried guns afeard o' the naygers, and in troth it's the hoight o' care he takes o' them same guns; and small blame to him, sure they might be the salvation of him.

'Pon my conscience, they 're taken betther care of than any poor man's child. I heerd him cautionin' the sailors about them, and givin' them ordhers about their clothes."

"Their clothes!" said his two companions at once, in much surprise; "is it clothes upon cannons?"

"It's thruth I 'm tellin' you," said Barny. "Bad luck to the lie in it, he was talkin' about their aprons and their breeches."

"O, think o' that!" said Jemmy and Peter, in surprise.

"An' 't was all iv a piece," said Barny, "that an' the rest o' the ship all out. She was as nate as a new pin. Throth, I was a'most ashamed to put my fut on the deck, it was so clane, and she painted every color in the rainbow; and all sorts o' curiosities about her; and instead iv a tiller to steer her, like this darlin' craythur iv ours, she goes wid a wheel, like a coach all as one; and there 's the quarest thing you iver seen, to show the way, as the captain gev me to understan', a little round rowly-powly thing in a bowl, that goes waddlin' about as if it did n't know its own way, much more nor show anybody theirs. Throth, myself thought that if that 's the way they 're obliged to go, that it 's with a great deal of fear and thrimblin' they find it out."

Thus it was that Barny continued most marvellous accounts of the ship and the captain to his companions, and by keeping their attention so engaged, prevented their being too inquisitive as to their own immediate concerns, and for two days more Barny and the hooker held on their respective courses undeviatingly.

The third day Barny's fears for the continuity of his *nor-aist coorse* were excited, as a large brig hove in sight, and the nearer she approached, the more directly she appeared to be coming athwart Barny's course.

"May the divil sweep you," said Barny, "and will nothin' else sarve you than comin' forninst me that away? Brig-a-hoy there!" shouted Barny, giving the tiller to one of his messmates, and standing at the bow of his boat. "Brig-a-hoy there! — bad luck to you, go 'long out o' my *nor-aist coorse*." The brig, instead of obeying him, hove to, and lay right ahead of the hooker. "O, look at this!" shouted Barny, and he stamped on the deck with rage, — "look at the blackguards where they're stayin', just a-purpose to ruin an unfortunate man like me. My heavy hathred to you, quit this minit, or I'll run down an yes, and if we go to the bottom, we'll haunt you forevermore, — go 'long out o' that, I tell you. The curse o' Crummil on you, you stupid vagabones, that won't go out iv a man's nor-aist coorse!"

From cursing Barny went to praying as he came closer. "For the tendher marcy o' heaven an' lave my way. May the Lord reward you, and get out o' my nor-aist coorse! May angels make your bed in heavin and don't ruinate me this a way." The brig was immovable, and Barny finished with a duet volley of prayers and curses together, apostrophizing the hard case of a man being "done out o' his nor-aist coorse."

"A-hoy there!" shouted a voice from the brig, "put down your helm or you'll be aboard of us. I say, let go your jib and foresheet, — what are you about, you lubbers?"

'T was true that the brig lay so fair in Barny's course, that he would have been aboard, but that instantly the manœuvre above alluded to was put in practice on board the hooker; as she swept to destruction toward the heavy hull of the brig, he luffed up into the wind alongside her. A very pale and somewhat emaciated face appeared at the side, and addressed Barny.

"What brings you here?" was the question.

"Throth, thin, and I think I might betther ax what brings *you* here, right in the way o' my *nor-aist coorse*."

"Where do you come from?"

"From Kinsale; and you did n't come from a betther place, I go bail."

"Where are you bound to?"

"To Fingal."

"Fingal, — where's Fingal?"

"Why then, ain't you ashamed o' yourself an' not to know where Fingal is?"

"It is not in these seas."

"O, and that's all you know about it," says Barny.

"You 're a small craft to be so far at sea. I suppose you have provisions on board?"

"To be sure we have; throth if we had n't, this id be a bad place to go a beggin'."

"What have you eatable?"

"The finest o' scalpeens."

"What are scalpeens?"

"Why, you 're mighty ignorant intirely," said Barny; "why, scalpeens is pickled mackerel."

"Then you must give us some, for we have been out of everything eatable these three days; and even pickled fish is better than nothing."

It chanced that the brig was a West India trader, which unfavorable winds had delayed much beyond the expected period of time on her voyage, and though her water had not failed, everything eatable had been consumed, and the crew reduced almost to helplessness. In such a strait the arrival of Barny O'Reirdon and his scalpeens was a most providential succor to them, and a lucky chance for Barny, for he got in exchange for his pickled fish a handsome return of rum and sugar, much more than equivalent to their value. Barny lamented much, however, that the brig was not bound for Ireland, that he might practice his own peculiar system of navigation; but as staying with the brig could do no good, he got himself put into his *nor-aist coorse* once more, and ploughed away toward home.

The disposal of his cargo was a great godsend to Barny in more ways than one. In the first place, he found the most profitable market he could have had; and, secondly, it enabled him to cover his retreat from the difficulty which still was before him of not getting to Fingal after all his dangers, and consequently being open to discovery and disgrace. All these beneficial results were thrown away upon one of Barny's readiness to avail himself of every point in his favor: and, accordingly, when they left the brig, Barny said to his companions, "Why, thin, boys, 'pon my conscience, but I 'm as proud as a horse wid a wooden leg this minit, that we met them poor unfort'nate craythers this blessed day, and was enabled to extind our charity to them. Sure, an' it's lost they'd be only for our comin' acrass them, and we, through the blessin' o' God, enabled to do an act o' marcy, that is, feedin' the hungry; and sure every good work we do here is before uz in heaven,—and that's a comfort anyhow. To be sure, now that the scalpeens is sowld, there's no use in goin' to Fingal, and we may as well jist go home."

"Faix, I'm sorry myself," said Jemmy, "for Terry O'Sullivan said it was an iligant place intirely, an' I wanted to see it."

"To the divil wid Terry O'Sullivan," said Barny; "how does he know what's an iligant place? What knowledge has he of iligance! I'll go bail he never was half as far a navigatin' as we,—he wint the short cut, I go bail, and never dar'd for to vinture the round, as I did."

"By dad, we wor a great dale longer anyhow than he towld me he was."

"To be sure we wor," said Barny; "he wint skulkin' in by the short cut, I tell you, and was afeard to keep a bowld offin' like me. But come, boys, let uz take a dhrop o' the bottle o' sper'ts we got out o' the brig. By gor, it's well we got some bottles iv it; for I would n't much like to meddle wid that darlint little kag iv it antil we get home." The rum was put on its trial by Barny and his companions, and in their critical judgment was pronounced quite as good as the captain of the ship had bestowed upon them, but that neither of those specimens of spirit was to be compared to whiskey.

"By dad," says Barny, "they may rack their brains a

long time before they'll make out a purtier invintion than *potteen*, — that rum may do very well for thim that has the misforthin' not to know betther; but the whiskey is a more nathral sper't accordin' to my idays." In this, as in most other of Barny's opinions, Peter and Jemmy coincided.

Nothing particular occurred for the two succeeding days, during which time Barny most religiously pursued his *nor-aist coorse*, but the third day produced a new and important event. A sail was discovered on the horizon, and in the direction Barny was steering, and a couple of hours made him tolerably certain that the vessel in sight was an American, for though it is needless to say that he was not very conversant in such matters, yet from the frequency of his seeing Americans trading to Ireland, his eye had become sufficiently accustomed to their lofty and tapering spars, and peculiar smartness of rig, to satisfy him that the ship before him was of transatlantic build; nor was he wrong in his conjecture.

Barny now determined on a manœuvre, classing him among the first tacticians at securing a good retreat.

Moreau's highest fame rests upon his celebrated retrograde movement through the Black Forest.

Xenophon's greatest glory is derived from the deliverance of his ten thousand Greeks from impending ruin by his renowned retreat.

Let the ancient and the modern hero " repose under the shadow of their laurels," as the French have it, while Barny O'Reirdon's historian, with a pardonable jealousy for the honor of his country, cuts down a goodly bough of the classic tree, beneath which our Hibernian hero may enjoy his *otium cum dignitate.*

Barny calculated the American was bound for Ireland, and as she lay *almost* as directly in the way of his "nor-aist coorse" as the West-Indian brig, he bore up to and spoke her.

He was answered by a shrewd Yankee captain.

"Faix, an' it's glad I am to see your honor again," said Barny.

The Yankee had never been to Ireland, and told Barny so.

"O, throth, I couldn't forget a gintleman so aisy as that," said Barny.

"You're pretty considerably mistaken now, I guess," said the American.

"Divil a taste," said Barny, with inimitable composure and pertinacity.

"Well, if you know me so tarnation well, tell me what's my name." The Yankee flattered himself he had nailed Barny now.

"Your name, is it?" said Barny, gaining time by repeating the question; "why, what a fool you are not to know your own name."

The oddity of the answer posed the American, and Barny took advantage of the diversion in his favor, and changed the conversation.

"By dad, I've been waitin' here these four or five days, expectin' some of you would be wantin' me."

"Some of us! — How do you mean?"

"Sure, an' ar'n't you from Amerikay?"

"Yes; and what then?"

"Well, I say I was waitin' for some ship or other from Amerikay, that ud be wantin' me. It's to Ireland you're goin'?"

"Yes."

"Well, I suppose you'll be wantin' a pilot," said Barny.

"Yes, when we get in shore, but not yet."

"O, I don't want to hurry you," said Barny.

"What port are you a pilot of?"

"Why, indeed, as for the matther o' that," said Barny, "they're all aiqual to me a'most."

"All?" said the American. "Why, I calculate you couldn't pilot a ship into all the ports of Ireland."

"Not all at wanst," said Barny, with a laugh, in which the American could not help joining.

"Well, I say, what ports do you know best?"

"Why, thin, indeed," said Barny, "it would be hard for me to tell; but wherever you want to go, I'm the man that'll do the job for you complate. Where is your honor goin'?"

"I won't tell you that, — but do you tell me what ports you know best?"

"Why, there's Watherford, and there's Youghal, an' Fingal."

"Fingal, — where's that?"

"So you don't know where Fingal is. O, I see you're a sthranger, sir, — an' then there's Cork."

"You know Cove, then?"

"Is it the Cove o' Cork?"

"Yes."

"I was bred and born there, and pilots as many ships into Cove as any other two min *out* of it."

Barny thus sheltered his falsehood under the idiom of his language.

"But what brought you so far out to sea?" asked the captain.

"We wor lyin' out lookin' for ships that wanted pilots, and there kem an the terriblest gale o' wind aff the land, an' blew us to say out intirely, an' that's the way iv it, your honor."

"I calculate we got a share of the same gale; 't was from the nor-east."

"O, directly!" said Barny, "faith, you're right enough. 'T was the *nor-aist coorse* we wor an sure enough; but no matther now that we've met wid you, — sure we'll have a job home anyhow."

"Well, get aboard then," said the American.

"I will, in a minit, your honor, whin I jist spake a word to my comrades here."

"Why, sure it's not goin' to turn pilot you are," said Jemmy, in his simplicity of heart.

"Whisht, you omadhaun!" said Barny, "or I'll cut the tongue out o' you. Now mind me, Pether. You don't undherstan' navigashin and the varrious branches o' knowledge, an' so all you have to do is to folly the ship when I get into her, an' I'll show you the way home."

Barny then got aboard the American vessel, and begged of the captain, that as he had been out at sea so long, and had gone through "a power o' hardship intirely," he would be permitted to go below and turn in to take a sleep, "for in throth it's myself and sleep that is sthrayngers for some time," said Barny, "an' if your honor 'll be plazed I 'll be thankful if you won't let them disturb me antil I 'm wanted, for sure till you see the land there's no use for me in life, an' throth I want a sleep sorely."

Barny's request was granted, and it will not be wondered at, that after so much fatigue of mind and body, he slept profoundly for four-and-twenty hours. He then was called, for land was in sight, and when he came on deck the captain rallied him upon the potency of his somniferous qualities, and " calculated " he had never met any one who could sleep " four-and-twenty hours at a stretch before."

"O sir," said Barny, rubbing his eyes, which were still a little hazy, " whiniver I go to sleep I pay attintion to it."

The land was soon neared, and Barny put in charge of the ship, when he ascertained the first landmark he was acquainted with; but as soon as the Head of Kinsale hove in sight, Barny gave a "whoo," and cut a caper that astonished the Yankees, and was quite inexplicable to them, though, I flatter myself, it is not to those who do Barny the favor of reading his adventures.

"O, there you are, my darlint ould head! An' where's the head like o' you? Throth, it 's little I thought I 'd ever set eyes an your good-looking faytures agin. But God 's good!"

In such half-muttered exclamations, did Barny apostrophize each well-known point of his native shore, and when opposite the harbor of Kinsale, he spoke the hooker that was somewhat astern, and ordered Jemmy and Peter to put in there, and tell Molly immediately that he was come back, and would be with her as soon as he could, after piloting the ship into Cove. "But an your apperl don't tell Pether Kelly o' the big farm, nor, indeed, don't mintion to man or mortial about the navigation we done antil I come home myself and make them sensible o' it, bekase, Jemmy and Pether, neither o' yiz is aqual to it, and does n't undherstan' the branches o' knowledge requizit for discoorsin' o' navigation."

The hooker put into Kinsale, and Barny sailed the ship into Cove. It was the first ship he ever had acted the pilot for, and his old luck attended him; no accident befell his charge, and, what was still more extraordinary, he made the American believe he was absolutely the most skilful pilot on the station. So Barny pocketed his pilot's fee, swore the Yankee was a gentleman, for which the republican did not thank him, wished him good by, and then pushed his way home with what Barny swore was the aisiest-made money he ever had in his life. So Barny got himself paid for piloting the ship that showed him the way home.

HADDAD-BEN-AHAB THE TRAVELLER.

BY JOHN GALT.

HADDAD-BEN-AHAB was a very wise man, and he had several friends, men of discernment, and partakers of the wisdom of ages; but they were not all so wise as Haddad-Ben-Ahab. His sentences were short, but his knowledge was long, and what he predicted generally came to pass, for he did not pretend to the gift of prophecy. The utmost he ever said in that way was, that he expected the sun to rise to-morrow, and that old age was the shadow of youth.

Besides being of a grave temperament, Haddad-Ben-Ahab was inclined to obesity; he was kindly and good-natured to the whole human race; he even carried his benevolence to the inferior creation, and often patted his dogs on the head and gave them bones; but cats he could not abide. Had he been a rat he could not have regarded them with more antipathy; and yet Haddad-Ben-Ahab was an excellent man, who smoked his chibouque with occasional cups of coffee and sherbet, interspersed with profound aphorisms on the condition of man, and conjectures on the delights of paradise.

With his friends he passed many sunbright hours; and if much talk was not heard among them on these occasions, be it remembered that silence is often wisdom. The scene of their social resort was a little kiosk in front of one of the coffee-houses on the bank of the Tigris. No place in all Bagdad is so pleasantly situated. There the mighty river rolls in all the affluence of his waters, pure as the unclouded sky, and speckled with innumerable boats, while the rippling waves, tickled, as it were, by the summer breezes, gambol and sparkle around.

The kiosk was raised two steps from the ground; the interior was painted with all the most splendid colors. The roof was covered with tiles that glittered like the skin of the Arabian serpent, and was surmounted with a green dragon, which was painted of that imperial hue, because Haddad-Ben-Ahab was descended from the sacred progeny of Fatima, of whom green is the everlasting badge, as it is of nature. Time cannot change it, nor can it be impaired by the decrees of tyranny or of justice.

One beautiful day Haddad-Ben-Ahab and his friends had met in this kiosk of dreams, and were socially enjoying the fragrant smoke of their pipes, and listening to the refreshing undulations of the river, as the boats softly glided along, — for the waters lay in glassy stillness, — the winds were asleep, — even the sunbeams seemed to rest in a slumber on all things. The smoke stood on the chimney-tops as if a tall visionary tree grew out of each; and the many-colored cloths in the yard of Orooblis, the Armenian dyer, hung unmolested by a breath. Orooblis himself was the only thing, in that soft and bright noon, which appeared on the land to be animated with any purpose.

Orooblis was preparing a boat to descend the Tigris, and his servants were loading it with bales of apparel and baskets of provisions, while he himself was in a great bustle, going often between his dwelling-house and the boat, talking loud and giving orders, and ever and anon wiping his forehead, for he was a man that delighted in having an ado.

Haddad-Ben-Ahab, seeing Orooblis so active, looked at him for some time; and it so happened that all the friends at the same moment took their amber-headed pipes from their lips, and said, —

"Where can Orooblis, the Armenian dyer, be going?"

Such a simultaneous interjection naturally surprised them all, and Haddad-Ben-Ahab added, —

"I should like to go with him, and see strange things, for I have never been out of the city of Bagdad, save once to pluck pomegranates in the garden of Beys-Addy-Boolk." And he then rose and went to the boat which Orooblis was loading, and spoke to him; and when it was ready they seated themselves on board and sailed down the Tigris, having much pleasant discourse concerning distant lands and hills whose tops pierced the clouds, and were supposed to be the pillars that upheld the crystal dome of the heavens.

Haddad-Ben-Ahab rejoiced greatly as they sailed along, and at last they came to a little town, where Orooblis, having business in dyestuffs to transact, went on shore, leaving his friend. But in what corner of the earth this little town stood Haddad-Ben-Ahab knew not;

for, like other travellers, he was not provided with much geographical knowledge.

But soon after the departure of Orooblis he thought he would also land and inquire. Accordingly, taking his pipe in his hand, he stepped out of the boat and went about the town, looking at many things, till he came to a wharf where a large ship was taking merchandise on board; and her sailors were men of a different complexion from that of the watermen who plied on the Tigris at Bagdad.

Haddad-Ben-Ahab looked at them, and as he was standing near to where they were at work, he thought that this ship afforded a better opportunity than he had enjoyed with Orooblis to see foreign countries. He accordingly went up to the captain and held out a handful of money, and indicated that he was desirous to sail away with the ship.

When the captain saw the gold he was mightily civil, and spoke to Haddad-Ben-Ahab with a loud voice, perhaps thinking to make him hear was the way to make him understand. But Haddad-Ben-Ahab only held up the forefinger of his right hand and shook it to and fro. In the end, however, he was taken on board the ship, and no sooner was he there than he sat down on a sofa, and drawing his legs up under him kindled his pipe and began to smoke, much at his ease, making observations with his eyes as he did so.

The first observation Haddad-Ben-Ahab made was, that the sofa on which he had taken his place was not at all like the sofas of Bagdad, and therefore when he returned he would show that he had not travelled without profit by having one made exactly similar for his best chamber, with hens and ducks under it, pleasantly feeding and joyously cackling and quacking. And he also observed a remarkable sagacity in the ducks, for when they saw he was a stranger, they turned up the sides of their heads and eyed him in a most curious and inquisitive manner, — very different, indeed, from the ducks of Bagdad.

When the ship had taken on board her cargo she spread her sails, and Haddad-Ben-Ahab felt himself in a new situation; for presently she began to lie over, and to plunge and revel among the waves like a glad creature. But Haddad-Ben-Ahab became very sick, and the captain showed him the way down into the inside of the vessel, where he went into a dark bed, and was charitably tended by one of the sailors for many days.

After a season there was much shouting on the deck of the ship, and Haddad-Ben-Ahab crawled out of his bed, and went to the sofa, and saw that the ship was near the end of her voyage.

When she had come to a bank where those on board could step out, Haddad-Ben-Ahab did so: and after he had seen all the strange things which were in the town where he thus landed, he went into a baker's shop, — for they eat bread in that town as they do in Bagdad, — and bought a loaf, which having eaten, he quenched his thirst at a fountain hard by, in his ordinary manner of drinking, at which he wondered exceedingly.

When he had solaced himself with all the wonders of that foreign city, he went to a fakier, who was holding two horses ready saddled; beautiful they were, and, as the fakier signified by signs, their hoofs were so fleet that they left the wind behind them. Haddad-Ben-Ahab then showed the fakier his gold, and mounted one of the horses, pointing with the shaft of his pipe to the fakier to mount the other; and then they both rode away into the country, and they found that the wind blew in their faces.

At last they came to a caravansary, where the fakier bought a cooked hen and two onions, of which they both partook, and stretching themselves before the fire which they had lighted in their chamber, they fell asleep and slept until the dawn of day, when they resumed their journey into remoter parts and nearer to the wall of the world, which Haddad-Ben-Ahab conjectured they must soon reach. They had not, however, journeyed many days in the usual manner when they came to the banks of a large river, and the fakier would go no farther with his swift horses. Haddad-Ben-Ahab was in consequence constrained to pay and part from him, and to embark in a ferry-boat to convey him over the stream, where he found a strange vehicle with four horses standing ready to carry him on towards the wall of the world, "which surely," said he to himself, "ought not to be now far off."

Haddad-Ben-Ahab showed his gold again, and was permitted to take a seat in the vehicle, which soon after drove away; and he remarked, in a most sagacious manner, that nothing in that country was like the things in his own; for the houses and trees and all things ran away as the vehicle came up to them; and when it gave a jostle, they gave a jump; which he noted as one of the most extraordinary things he had seen since he left Bagdad.

At last Haddad-Ben-Ahab came to the foot of a lofty green mountain, with groves and jocund villages, which studded it, as it were, with gems and shining ornaments, and he said, "This must be the wall of the world, for surely nothing can exist on the other side of these hills! but I will ascend them and look over, for I should like to tell my friends in Bagdad what is to be seen on the outside of the earth." Accordingly he ascended the green mountain, and he came to a thick forest of stubby trees: "This is surprising," said Haddad-Ben-Ahab, "but higher I will yet go." And he passed through that forest of trees and came to a steep moorland part of the hill, where no living thing could be seen, but a solitude without limit, and the living world all glittering at the foot of the mountain.

"This is a high place," said Haddad-Ben-Ahab, "but I will yet go higher," and he began to climb with his hands. After an upward journey of great toil he came to a frozen region, and the top of the wall of the world was still far above him. He was, however, none daunted by the distance, but boldly held on in the ascent, and at last he reached the top of the wall. But when he got there, instead of a region of fog and chaos, he only beheld another world much like our own, and he was greatly amazed, and exclaimed with a loud voice, — "Will my friends in Bagdad believe this? — but it is true, and I will so tell them." So he hastened down the mountain, and went with all the speed he could back to Bagdad; saying, "Bagdad," and giving gold to every man he met, until he reached the kiosk of dreams, where his friends were smoking and looking at the gambols of the Tigris.

When the friends of Haddad-Ben-Ahab saw him approach, they respectively took their pipes from their mouths and held them in their left hands, while they pressed their bosoms with their right, and received him with a solemn salaam, for he had been long absent, and all they in the mean time had heard concerning him was only what Orooblis, the Armenian dyer, on his return told them: namely, that he was gone to the wall of the world, which limits the travels of man. No wonder then that they rejoiced with an exceeding gladness to see him return and take his place in the kiosk among them, as if he had never been a day's journey away from Bagdad.

They then questioned him about his adventures, and he faithfully related to them all the wonders which have been set forth in our account of the journey; upon which they declared he had made himself one of the sages of the earth.

Afterward they each made a feast, to which they invited all the philosophers in Bagdad, and Haddad-Ben-Ahab was placed in the seat of honor, and being courteously solicited, told them of his travels, and every one cried aloud, "God is great, and Mahomet is his prophet!"

When they had in this manner banqueted, Haddad-Ben-Ahab fell sick, and there was a great talk concerning the same. Some said he was very ill; others shook their heads and spoke not; but the world is full of envy and hard-heartedness, and those who were spiteful because of the renown which Haddad-Ben-Ahab, as a traveller who had visited the top of the wall of the world with so much courage, had acquired, jeered at his malady, saying he had been only feasted overmuch. Nevertheless, Haddad-Ben-Ahab died; and never was such a funeral seen in all Bagdad, save that of the caliph Mahoud, commonly called the Magnificent. Such was the admiration in which the memory of the traveller was held, the poets made dirges on the occasion, and mournful songs were heard in the twilight from the windows of every harem. Nor did the generation of the time content itself with the ceremonies of lamentation: they caused a fountain to be erected, which they named the Fountain of Haddad-Ben-Ahab the traveller; and when the slaves go to fetch water, they speak of the wonderful things he did, and how he was on the top of the wall of the world, and saw the outside of the earth; so that his memory lives forever among them, as one of the greatest, the wisest, and the bravest of men.

BLUEBEARD'S GHOST.

BY WILLIAM MAKEPEACE THACKERAY.

FOR some time after the fatal accident which deprived her of her husband, Mrs. Bluebeard was, as may be imagined, in a state of profound grief.

There was not a widow in all the country who went to such an expense for black bombazine. She had her beautiful hair confined in crimped caps, and her weepers came over her elbows. Of course, she saw no company except her sister Anne (whose company was anything but pleasant to the widow); as for her brothers, their odious mess-table manners had always been disagreeable to her. What did she care for jokes about the major, or scandal concerning the Scotch surgeon of the regiment? If they drank their wine out of black bottles or crystal, what did it matter to her? Their stories of the stable, the parade, and the last run with the hounds, were perfectly odious to her; besides, she could not bear their impertinent mustachios, and filthy habit of smoking cigars.

They were always wild, vulgar young men, at the

best; but now, — *now*, O, their presence to her delicate soul was horror! How could she bear to look on them after what had occurred? She thought of the best of husbands ruthlessly cut down by their cruel, heavy, cavalry sabres; the kind friend, the generous landlord, the spotless justice of peace, in whose family differences these rude cornets of dragoons had dared to interfere, whose venerable blue hairs they had dragged down with sorrow to the grave.

She put up a most splendid monument to her departed lord over the family vault of the Bluebeards. The rector, Dr. Sly, who had been Mr. Bluebeard's tutor at college, wrote an epitaph in the most pompous yet pathetic Latin: "Siste, viator! mœrens conjux, heu! quanto minus est cum reliquis versari quam tui meminisse"; in a word, everything that is usually said in epitaphs. A bust of the departed saint, with Virtue mourning over it, stood over the epitaph, surrounded by medallions of his wives, and one of these medallions had as yet no name in it, nor (the epitaph said) could the widow ever be consoled until her own name was inscribed there. "For then I shall be with him. In cœlo quies," she would say, throwing up her fine eyes to heaven, and quoting the enormous words of the hatchment which was put up in the church, and over Bluebeard's hall, where the butler, the housekeeper, the footman, the housemaid, and scullions were all in the profoundest mourning. The keeper went out to shoot birds in a crape band; nay, the very scarecrows in the orchard and fruit garden were ordered to be dressed in black.

Sister Anne was the only person who refused to wear black. Mrs. Bluebeard would have parted with her, but she had no other female relative. Her father, it may be remembered by readers of the former part of her Memoirs, had married again, and the mother-in-law and Mrs. Bluebeard, as usual, hated each other furiously. Mrs. Shacabac had come to the hall on a visit of condolence; but the widow was so rude to her on the second day of the visit that the step-mother quitted the house in a fury. As for the Bluebeards, of course *they* hated the widow. Had not Mr. Bluebeard settled every shilling upon her? and, having no children by his former marriage, her property, as I leave you to fancy, was pretty handsome. So Sister Anne was the only female relative whom Mrs. Bluebeard would keep near her; and, as we all know, a woman *must* have a female relative under any circumstances of pain, or pleasure, or profit, — when she is married, or when she is widowed, or when she is in a delicate situation. But let us continue our story.

"I will never wear mourning for that odious wretch, sister!" Anne would cry.

"I will trouble you, Miss Anne, not to use such words in my presence regarding the best of husbands, or to quit the room at once!" the widow would answer.

"I'm sure it's no great pleasure to sit in it. I wonder you don't make use of the closet, sister, where the *other* Mrs. Bluebeards are."

"Impertinence! they were all embalmed by M. Gannal. How dare you report the monstrous calumnies regarding the best of men? Take down the family Bible, and read what my blessed saint says of his wives, — read it, written in his own hand: —

"'*Friday, June* 20. — Married my beloved wife, Anna Maria Scrogginsia.

"'*Saturday, August* 1. — A bereaved husband has scarcely strength to write down in this chronicle that the dearest of wives, Anna Maria Scrogginsia, expired this day of sore throat.'

"There! can anything be more convincing than that? Read again: —

"'*Tuesday, September* 1. — This day I led to the hymeneal altar my soul's blessing, Louisa Matilda Hopkinson. May this angel supply the place of her I have lost!

"'*Wednesday, October* 5. — O Heavens! pity the distraction of a wretch who is obliged to record the ruin of his dearest hopes and affections! This day my adored Louisa Matilda Hopkinson gave up the ghost! A complaint of the head and shoulders was the sudden cause of the event which has rendered the unhappy subscriber the most miserable of men.
"'BLUEBEARD.'

"Every one of the women are calendared in this delightful, this pathetic, this truly virtuous and tender way; and can you suppose that a man who wrote such sentiments could be a *murderer*, miss?"

"Do you mean to say that he did not *kill* them, then?" said Anne.

"Gracious goodness, Anne, kill them! they died all as naturally as I hope you will. My blessed husband was an angel of goodness and kindness to them.

Was it *his* fault that the doctors could not cure their maladies? No, that it wasn't! and when they died the inconsolable husband had their bodies embalmed in order that on this side of the grave he might never part from them."

"And why did he take you up in the tower, pray? And why did you send me in such a hurry to the leads? and why did he sharpen his long knife, and roar out to you to COME DOWN?"

"Merely to punish me for my curiosity, — the dear, good, kind, excellent creature!" sobbed the widow, overpowered with affectionate recollections of her lord's attentions to her.

"I wish," said Sister Anne, sulkily, "that I had not been in such a hurry in summoning my brothers."

"Ah!" screamed Mrs. Bluebeard, with a harrowing scream, "don't, — don't recall that horrid, fatal day, miss! If you had not misled your brothers, my poor, dear, darling Bluebeard would still be in life, still — still the soul's joy of his bereaved Fatima!"

Whether it is that all wives adore husbands when the latter are no more, or whether it is that Fatima's version of the story is really the correct one, and that the common impression against Bluebeard is an odious prejudice, and that he no more murdered his wives than you and I have, remains yet to be proved, and, indeed, does not much matter for the understanding of the rest of Mrs. B.'s adventures. And though people will say that Bluebeard's settlement of his whole fortune on his wife, in event of survivorship, was a mere act of absurd mystification, seeing that he was fully determined to cut her head off after the honeymoon, yet the best test of his real intentions is the profound grief which the widow manifested for his death, and the fact that he left her mighty well to do in the world.

If any one were to leave you or me a fortune, my dear friend, would we be too anxious to rake up the how and the why? Pooh! pooh! we would take it and make no bones about it, and Mrs. Bluebeard did likewise. Her husband's family, it is true, argued the point with her, and said, "Madam, you must perceive that Mr. Bluebeard never intended the fortune for you, as it was his fixed intention to chop off your head! It is clear that he meant to leave his money to his blood relations, therefore you ought in equity to hand it over. But she sent them all off with a flea in their ears, as the saying is, and said, "Your argument may be a very good one, but I will, if you please, keep the money." And she ordered the mourning as we have before shown, and indulged in grief, and exalted everywhere the character of the deceased. If any one would but leave me a fortune, what a funeral and what a character I would give him!

Bluebeard Hall is situated, as we all very well know, in a remote country district, and, although a fine residence, is remarkably gloomy and lonely. To the widow's susceptible mind, after the death of her darling husband, the place became intolerable. The walk, the lawn, the fountain, the green glades of park over which frisked the dappled deer, all, — all recalled the memory of her beloved. It was but yesterday that, as they roamed through the park in the calm summer evening, her

Bluebeard pointed out to the keeper the fat buck he was to kill. "Ah!" said the widow, with tears in her fine eyes, "the artless stag was shot down, the haunch was cut and roasted, the jelly had been prepared from the currant-bushes in the garden that he loved, but my Bluebeard never ate of the venison! Look, Anne sweet, pass we the old oak hall; 't is hung with trophies won by him in the chase, with pictures of the noble race of Bluebeard! Look! by the fireplace there is the gig-whip, his riding-whip, the spud with which you know he used to dig the weeds out of the terrace-walk; in that drawer are his spurs, his whistle, his visiting-cards, with his dear, dear name engraven upon them! There are the bits of string that he used to cut off the parcels and keep, because string was always useful; his button-hook, and there is the peg on which he used to hang his h—h—*hat!*"

Uncontrollable emotions, bursts of passionate tears, would follow these tender reminiscences of the widow; and the long and short of the matter was, that she was determined to give up Bluebeard Hall and live elsewhere; her love for the memory of the deceased, she said, rendered the place too wretched.

Of course, an envious and sneering world said that she was tired of the country, and wanted to marry again; but she little heeded its taunts; and Anne, who hated her step-mother and could not live at home, was fain to accompany her sister to the town where the Bluebeards have had for many years a very large, genteel, old-fashioned house. So she went to the town-house, where they lived and quarrelled pretty much as usual; and though Anne often threatened to leave her, and go to a boarding-house, of which there were plenty in the place, yet, after all, to live with her sister, and drive out in the carriage with the footman and coachman in mourning, and the lozenge on the panels, with the Bluebeard and Shacabac arms quartered on it, was far more respectable, and so the lovely sisters continued to dwell together.

For a lady under Mrs. Bluebeard's circumstances, the town-house has other and peculiar advantages. Besides being an exceedingly spacious and dismal brick building, with a dismal iron railing in front, and long, dismal, thin windows, with little panes of glass, it looked out into the churchyard, where, time out of mind, between two yew-trees, one of which is cut into the form of a peacock, while the other represents a dumb-waiter, it looked into the churchyard where the monument of the late Bluebeard was placed over the family vault. It was the first thing the widow saw from her bedroom window in the morning, and 'twas sweet to watch at night, from the parlor, the pallid moonlight lighting up the bust of the departed, and Virtue throwing great black shadows athwart it. Polyanthuses, rhododendra, ranunculuses, and other flowers, with the largest names and of the most delightful odors, were planted within the little iron railing that enclosed the last resting-place of the Bluebeards; and the beadle was instructed to half kill any little boys who might be caught plucking these sweet testimonials of a wife's affection.

Over the sideboard in the dining-room hung a full-length of Mr. Bluebeard, by Ticklegill, R. A., in a militia uniform, frowning down upon the knives and forks and silver trays. Over the mantel-piece he was represented in a hunting costume, on his favorite horse; there was a sticking-plaster silhouette of him in the widow's bedroom, and a miniature in the drawing-room, where he was drawn in a gown of black and gold, holding a gold-tasselled trencher cap with one hand, and with the other pointing to a diagram of Pons Asinorum. This likeness was taken when he was a fellow-commoner at St. John's College, Cambridge, and before the growth of that blue beard which was the ornament of his manhood, and a part of which now formed a beautiful blue neck-chain for his bereaved wife.

Sister Anne said the town-house was even more dismal than the country-house, for there was pure air at the Hall, and it was pleasanter to look out on a park than on a churchyard, however fine the monuments might be. But the widow said she was a light-minded hussy, and persisted as usual in her lamentations and mourning. The only male whom she would admit within her doors was the parson of the parish, who read sermons to her; and, as his reverence was at least seventy years old, Anne, though she might be ever so much minded to fall in love, had no opportunity to indulge her inclination; and the town-people, scandalous as they might be, could not find a word to say against the *liaison* of the venerable man and the heart-stricken widow.

All other company she resolutely refused. When the players were in the town, the poor manager, who came to beg her to bespeak a comedy, was thrust out of the gates by the big butler. Though there were balls, card-parties, and assemblies, Widow Bluebeard would never subscribe to one of them; and even the officers, those all-conquering heroes who make such ravages in ladies' hearts, and to whom all ladies' doors are commonly open, could never get an entry into the widow's house. Captain Whiskerfield strutted for three weeks up and down before her house, and had not the least effect upon her. Captain O'Grady (of an Irish regiment) attempted to bribe the servants, and one night actually scaled the garden wall; but all that he got was his foot in a man-trap, not to mention being dreadfully scarified by the broken glass; and so *he* never made love any more. Finally, Captain Blackbeard, whose whiskers vied in magnitude with those of the deceased Bluebeard himself, although he attended church regularly every week, — he who had not darkened the doors of a church for ten years before, — even Captain Blackbeard got nothing by his piety; and the widow never once took her eyes off her book to look at him. The barracks were in despair; and Captain Whiskerfield's tailor, who had supplied him with new clothes in order to win the widow's heart, ended by clapping the captain into jail.

His reverence the parson highly applauded the widow's conduct to the officers; but, being himself rather of a social turn, and fond of a good dinner and a bottle, he represented to the lovely mourner that she should endeavor to divert her grief by a little respectable society, and recommended that she should from time to time entertain a few grave and sober persons whom he would present to her. As Dr. Sly had an unbounded influence over the fair mourner, she acceded to his desires; and accordingly he introduced to her house some of the most venerable and worthy of his acquaintance, — all married people, however, so that the widow should not take the least alarm.

It happened that the doctor had a nephew, who was a lawyer in London, and this gentleman came dutifully in the long vacation to pay a visit to his reverend uncle. "He is none of your roystering, dashing young fellows," said his reverence; "he is the delight of his mamma and sisters; he never drinks anything stronger than tea; he never missed church thrice a Sunday for these twenty years; and I hope, my dear and amiable madam, that you will not object to receive this pattern of young men for the sake of your most devoted friend, his uncle."

The widow consented to receive Mr. Sly. He was not a handsome man, certainly. "But what does that matter?" said the doctor. "He is *good*, and virtue is better than all the beauty of all the dragoons in the Queen's service."

Mr. Sly came there to dinner, and he came to tea; and he drove out with the widow in the carriage with the lozenge on it; and at church he handed the psalm-book; and, in short, he paid her every attention which could be expected from so polite a young gentleman.

At this the town began to talk, as people in towns will. "The doctor kept all bachelors out of the widow's house," said they, "in order that that ugly nephew of his may have the field entirely to himself." These speeches were of course heard by Sister Anne, and the little minx was not a little glad to take advantage of them, in order to induce her sister to see some more cheerful company. The fact is, the young hussy loved a dance or a game at cards much more than a humdrum conversation over a tea-table; and so she plied her sister day and night with hints as to the propriety of opening her house, receiving the gentry of the county, and spending her fortune.

To this point the widow at length, though with many sighs and vast unwillingness, acceded; and she went so far as to order a very becoming half-mourning, in which all the world declared she looked charming. "I carry," said she, "my blessed Bluebeard in my heart, — *that* is in the deepest mourning for him, and when the heart grieves, there is no need of outward show."

So she issued cards for a little quiet tea and supper, and several of the best families in the town and neighborhood attended her entertainment. It was followed by another and another; and at last Captain Blackbeard was actually introduced, though, of course, he came in plain clothes.

Dr. Sly and his nephew never could abide the captain. "They had heard some queer stories," they said, "about proceedings in barracks. Who was it that drank three bottles at a sitting? who had a mare that ran for the plate? and why was it that Dolly Coddlins left the town so suddenly?" Mr. Sly turned up the whites of his eyes as his uncle asked these questions, and sighed for the wickedness of the world. But for all that he was delighted, especially at the anger which the widow manifested when the Dolly Coddlins affair was hinted at. She was furious, and vowed she would never see the wretch again. The lawyer and his uncle were charmed. O short-sighted lawyer and parson, do you think Mrs. Bluebeard would have been so angry if she had not been jealous?—do you think she would have been jealous if she had not... had not what? She protested that she no more cared for the captain than she did for one of her footmen; but the next time he called she would not condescend to say a word to him.

"My dearest Miss Anne," said the captain, as he met her in Sir Roger de Coverley (she herself was dancing with Ensign Trippet), "what is the matter with your lovely sister?"

"Dolly Coddlins is the matter," said Miss Anne. "Mr. Sly has told all." And she was down the middle in a twinkling.

The captain blushed so at this monstrous insinuation, that any one could see how incorrect it was. He made innumerable blunders in the dance, and was all the time casting such ferocious glances at Mr. Sly (who did not dance, but sat by the widow and ate ices), that his partner thought he was mad, and that Mr. Sly became very uneasy.

When the dance was over, he came to pay his respects to the widow, and, in so doing, somehow trod so violently on Mr. Sly's foot, that that gentleman screamed with pain, and presently went home. But though he was gone, the widow was not a whit more gracious to Captain Blackbeard. She requested Mr. Trippet to order her carriage that night, and went home without uttering one single word to Captain Blackbeard.

The next morning, and with a face of preternatural

longitude, the Rev. Dr. Sly paid a visit to the widow. "The wickedness and bloodthirstiness of the world," said he, "increase every day. O my dear madam, what monsters do we meet in it, — what wretches, what assassins, are allowed to go abroad! Would you believe it, that this morning, as my nephew was taking his peaceful morning-meal, one of the ruffians from the barracks presented himself with a challenge from Captain Blackbeard?"

"Is he hurt?" screamed the widow.

"No, my dear friend, my dear Frederick is not hurt. And O, what a joy it will be to him to think you have that tender solicitude for his welfare!"

"You know I have always had the highest respect for him," said the widow; who, when she screamed, was in truth thinking of somebody else. But the doctor did not choose to interpret her thoughts in that way, and gave all the benefit of them to his nephew.

"That anxiety, dearest madam, which you express for him emboldens me, encourages me, authorizes me, to press a point upon you which I am sure must have entered your thoughts ere now. The dear youth in whom you have shown such an interest lives but for you! Yes, fair lady, start not at hearing that his sole affections are yours; and with what pride shall I carry to him back the news that he is not indifferent to you!"

"Are they going to fight?" continued the lady, in a breathless state of alarm. "For Heaven's sake, dearest doctor, prevent the horrid, horrid meeting. Send for a magistrate's warrant; do anything; but do not suffer those misguided young men to cut each other's throats!"

"Fairest lady, I fly!" said the doctor, and went back to lunch quite delighted with the evident partiality Mrs. Bluebeard showed for his nephew. And Mrs. Bluebeard, not content with exhorting him to prevent the duel, rushed to Mr. Pound, the magistrate, informed him of the facts, got out warrants against both Mr. Sly and the captain, and would have put them into execution; but it was discovered that the former gentleman had abruptly left town, so that the constable could not lay hold of him.

It somehow, however, came to be generally known that the widow Bluebeard had declared herself in favor of Mr. Sly, the lawyer; that she had fainted when told her lover was about to fight a duel; finally, that she had accepted him, and would marry him as soon as the quarrel between him and the captain was settled. Dr. Sly, when applied to, hummed and ha'd, and would give no direct answer; but he denied nothing, and looked so knowing, that all the world was certain of the fact; and the county paper next week stated : —

"We understand that the lovely and wealthy Mrs. Bl—b—rd is about once more to enter the bands of wedlock with our distinguished townsman, Frederick S—y, Esq., of the Middle Temple, London. The learned gentleman left town in consequence of a dispute with a gallant son of Mars, which was likely to have led to warlike results, had not a magistrate's warrant intervened, when the captain was bound over to keep the peace."

In fact, as soon as the captain was so bound over, Mr. Sly came back, stating that he had quitted the town not to avoid a duel, — far from it, but to keep out of the way of the magistrates, and give the captain every facility. *He* had taken out no warrant; *he* had been perfectly ready to meet the captain; if others had been more prudent, it was not his fault. So he held up his head, and cocked his hat with the most determined air; and all the lawyers' clerks in the place were quite proud of their hero.

As for Captain Blackbeard, his rage and indignation may be imagined; a wife robbed from him, his honor put in question by an odious, lanky, squinting lawyer! He fell ill of a fever incontinently; and the surgeon was obliged to take a quantity of blood from him, ten times the amount of which he swore he would have out of the veins of the atrocious Sly.

The announcement in "The Mercury," however, filled the widow with almost equal indignation. "The widow of the gallant Bluebeard," she said, "marry an odious wretch who lives in dingy chambers in the Middle Temple! Send for Dr. Sly." The doctor came; she rated him soundly, asked him how he dared set abroad such calumnies concerning her; ordered him to send his nephew back to London at once; and as he valued her esteem, as he valued the next presentation to a fat living which lay in her gift, to contradict everywhere, and in the fullest terms, the wicked report concerning her.

"My dearest madam," said the doctor, pulling his longest face, "you shall be obeyed. The poor lad shall be acquainted with the fatal change in your sentiments!"

"Change in my sentiments, Dr. Sly!"

"With the destruction of his hopes, rather let me

say; and Heaven grant that the dear boy have strength to bear up against the misfortune which comes so suddenly upon him!"

The next day Sister Anne came with a face full of care to Mrs. Bluebeard. "O, that unhappy lover of yours!" said she.

"Is the captain unwell?" exclaimed the widow.

"No, it is the other," answered Sister Anne. "Poor, poor Mr. Sly! He made a will leaving you all, except five pounds a year to his laundress: he made his will, locked his door, took heart-rending leave of his uncle at night, and this morning was found hanging at his bedpost when Sambo, the black servant, took him up his water to shave. 'Let me be buried,' he said, 'with the pincushion she gave me and the locket containing her hair.' *Did* you give him a pincushion, sister? *did* you give him a locket with your hair?"

"It was only silver-gilt!" sobbed the widow; "and now, O Heavens! I have killed him!" The heart-rending nature of her sobs may be imagined; but they were abruptly interrupted by her sister.

"Killed him? — no such thing! Sambo cut him down when he was as black in the face as the honest negro himself. He came down to breakfast, and I leave you to fancy what a touching meeting took place between the nephew and the uncle."

"So much love!" thought the widow. "What a pity he squints so! If he would but get his eyes put straight, I might perhaps — " She did not finish the sentence: ladies often leave this sort of sentence in a sweet confusion.

But hearing some news regarding Captain Blackbeard, whose illness and blood-letting were described to her most pathetically, as well as accurately, by the Scotch surgeon of the regiment, her feelings of compassion towards the lawyer cooled somewhat; and when Dr. Sly called to know if she would condescend to meet the unhappy youth, she said in rather a *distrait* manner, that she wished him every happiness; that she had the highest regard and respect for him; that she besought him not to think any more of committing the dreadful crime which would have made her unhappy forever; *but* that she thought, for the sake of both parties, they had better not meet until Mr. Sly's feelings had grown somewhat more calm.

"Poor fellow! poor fellow!" said the doctor, "may he be enabled to bear his frightful calamity! I have taken away his razors from him, and Sambo, my man, never lets him out of his sight."

The next day, Mrs. Bluebeard thought of sending a friendly message to Dr. Sly's, asking for news of the health of his nephew; but, as she was giving her orders on that subject to John Thomas the footman, it happened that the captain arrived, and so Thomas was sent down stairs again. And the captain looked so delightfully interesting with his arm in a sling, and his beautiful black whiskers curling round a face which was paler than usual, that, at the end of two hours, the widow forgot the message altogether, and, indeed, I believe, asked the captain whether he would not stop and dine. Ensign Trippet came, too, and the party was very pleasant; and the military gentlemen laughed hugely at the idea of the lawyer having been cut off the bedpost by the black servant, and were so witty on the subject, that the widow ended by half believing that the bedpost and hanging scheme on the part of Mr. Sly was only a feint, — a trick to win her heart. Though this, to be sure, was not agreed to by the lady without a pang, for, *entre nous*, to hang one's self for a lady is no small compliment to her attractions, and, perhaps, Mrs. Bluebeard was rather disappointed at the notion that the hanging was not a *bona fide* strangulation.

However, presently her nerves were excited again; and she was consoled or horrified, as the case may be (the reader must settle the point according to his ideas and knowledge of womankind), — she was at any rate dreadfully excited by the receipt of a billet in the well-known clerk-like hand of Mr. Sly. It ran thus: —

"I saw you through your dining-room windows. You were hob-nobbing with Captain Blackbeard. You looked rosy and well. You smiled. You drank off the champagne at a single draught.

"I can bear it no more. Live on, smile on, and be happy. My ghost shall repine, perhaps, at your happiness with another, — but in life I should go mad were I to witness it.

"It is best that I should be gone.

"When you receive this, tell my uncle to drag the fishpond at the end of Bachelor's Acre. His black servant Sambo accompanies me, it is true. But Sambo shall perish with me should his obstinacy venture to restrain me from my purpose. I know the poor fellow's honesty well, but I also know my own despair.

"Sambo will leave a wife and seven children. Be kind to those orphan mulattoes for the sake of
"Frederick."

The widow gave a dreadful shriek, and interrupted the two captains, who were each just in the act of swallowing a bumper of claret. "Fly — fly — save him," she screamed; "save him, monsters, ere it is too late! Drowned! — Frederick! — Bachelor's Wa —" Syncope took place, and the rest of the sentence was interrupted.

Deucedly disappointed at being obliged to give up their wine, the two heroes seized their cocked hats, and went towards the spot which the widow in her wild exclamations of despair had sufficiently designated.

Trippet was for running to the fish-pond at the rate of ten miles an hour.

"Take it easy, my good fellow," said Captain Blackbeard; "running is unwholesome after dinner. And, if that squinting scoundrel of a lawyer *does* drown himself, I sha' n't sleep any the worse." So the two gentlemen walked very leisurely on towards the Bachelor's Walk; and, indeed, seeing on their way thither Major Macabaw looking out of the window at his quarters and smoking a cigar, they went up stairs to consult the major, as also a bottle of Schiedam he had.

"They come not!" said the widow, when restored to herself. "O Heavens! grant that Frederick is safe! Sister Anne, go up to the leads and look if anybody is coming." And up, accordingly, to the garrets Sister Anne mounted. "Do you see anybody coming, Sister Anne?"

"I see Dr. Drench's little boy," said Sister Anne; "he is leaving a pill and draught at Miss Molly Grub's."

"Dearest Sister Anne, don't you see any one coming?" shouted the widow once again.

"I see a flock of dust—no! a cloud of sheep. Pshaw! I see the London coach coming in. There are three outsides, and the guard has flung a parcel to Mrs. Jenkins's maid."

"Distraction! Look once more, Sister Anne."

"I see a crowd,—a shutter,—a shutter with a man on it,—a beadle,—forty little boys,—Gracious goodness! what *can* it be?" and down stairs tumbled Sister Anne, and was looking out of the parlor-window by her sister's side, when the crowd she had perceived from the garret passed close by them.

At the head walked the beadle, slashing about at the little boys.

Two scores of these followed and surrounded

A SHUTTER carried by four men.

On the shutter lay *Frederick!* He was ghastly pale; his hair was draggled over his face; his clothes stuck tight to him on account of the wet; streams of water gurgled down the shutter-sides. But he was not dead! He turned one eye round towards the window where Mrs. Bluebeard sat, and gave her a look which she never could forget.

Sambo brought up the rear of the procession. He was quite wet through; and, if anything would have put his hair out of curl, his ducking would have done so. But, as he was not a gentleman, he was allowed to walk home on foot, and, as he passed the widow's window, he gave her one dreadful glance with his goggling black eyes, and moved on, pointing with his hands to the shutter.

John Thomas the footman was instantly despatched to Dr. Sly's to have news of the patient. There was no shilly-shallying now. He came back in half an hour to say that Mr. Frederick flung himself into Bachelor's Acre fish-pond with Sambo, had been dragged out with difficulty, had been put to bed, and had a pint of white wine whey, and was pretty comfortable. "Thank Heaven!" said the widow, and gave John Thomas a seven-shilling piece, and sat down with a lightened heart to tea. "What a heart!" said she to Sister Anne. "And O, what a pity it is that he squints!"

Here the two captains arrived. They had not been to the Bachelor's Walk; they had remained at Major Macabaw's consulting the Schiedam. They had made up their minds what to say. "Hang the fellow! he will never have the pluck to drown himself," said Captain Blackbeard. "Let us argue on that, as we may safely."

"My sweet lady," said he, accordingly, "we have had the pond dragged. No Mr. Sly. And the fisherman who keeps the punt assures us that he has not been there all day."

"Audacious falsehood!" said the widow, her eyes flashing fire. "Go, heartless man! who dares to trifle thus with the feelings of a respectable and unprotected woman. Go, sir, you 're only fit for the love of a — Dolly — Coddlins!" She pronounced the *Coddlins* with a withering sarcasm that struck the captain aghast; and, sailing out of the room, she left her tea untasted, and did not wish either of the military gentlemen good night.

But, gentles, an' ye know the delicate fibre of woman's heart, ye will not in very sooth believe that such events as those we have described — such tempests of passion — fierce winds of woe — blinding lightnings of tremendous joy and tremendous grief — could pass over one frail flower and leave it all unscathed. No! Grief kills as joy doth. Doth not the scorching sun nip the rosebud as well as the bitter wind? As Mrs. Sigourney sweetly sings: —

> "Ah! the heart is a soft and a delicate thing;
> Ah! the heart is a lute with a thrilling string;
> A spirit that floats on a gossamer's wing!"

Such was Fatima's heart. In a word, the preceding events had a powerful effect upon her nervous system, and she was ordered much quiet and sal-volatile by her skilful medical attendant, Dr. Glauber.

To be so ardently, passionately loved as she was, to know that Frederick had twice plunged into death from attachment to her, was to awaken in her bosom " a thrilling string," indeed! Could she witness such attachment and not be touched by it? She *was* touched by it, — she was influenced by the virtues, by the passion, by the misfortunes, of Frederick: but then he was so abominably ugly that she could not — she could not consent to become his bride!

She told Dr. Sly so. "I respect and esteem your nephew," said she; "but my resolve is made. I will continue faithful to that blessed saint whose monument is ever before my eyes" (she pointed to the churchyard as she spoke). "Leave this poor tortured heart in quiet. It has already suffered more than most hearts could bear. I will repose under the shadow of that tomb until I am called to rest within it, — to rest by the side of my Bluebeard!"

The ranunculuses, rhododendra, and polyanthuses, which ornamented that mausoleum, had somehow been suffered to run greatly to seed during the last few months, and it was with no slight self-accusation that she acknowledged this fact on visiting "the garden of the grave," as she called it; and she scolded the beadle soundly for neglecting his duty towards it. He promised obedience for the future, dug out all the weeds that were creeping round the family vault, and (having charge of the key) entered that awful place, and swept and dusted the melancholy contents of the tomb.

Next morning, the widow came down to breakfast looking very pale. She had passed a bad night; she had had awful dreams; she had heard a voice call her thrice at midnight. "Pooh! my dear, it's only nervousness," said sceptical Sister Anne.

Here John Thomas, the footman, entered, and said the beadle was in the hall, looking in a very strange way. He had been about the house since daybreak, and insisted on seeing Mrs. Bluebeard. "Let him enter," said that lady, prepared for some great mystery. The beadle came; he was pale as death; his hair was dishevelled, and his cocked hat out of order. "What have you to say?" said the lady, trembling.

Before beginning, he fell down on his knees.

"Yesterday," said he, "according to your ladyship's orders, I dug up the flower-beds of the family vault, dusted the vault and the — the coffins (added he, trembling) inside. Me and John Sexton did it together, and polished up the plate quite beautiful."

"For Heaven's sake, don't allude to it," cried the widow, turning pale.

"Well, my lady, I locked the door, came away, and found in my hurry — for I wanted to beat two little boys what was playing at marbles on Alderman Paunch's monyment — I found, my lady, I'd forgot my cane.

"I couldn't get John Sexton to go back with me till this morning, and I didn't like to go alone, and so we went this morning; and what do you think I found? I found his honor's coffin turned round, and the cane broke in two. Here's the cane!"

"Ah!" screamed the widow, "take it away, — take it away!"

"Well, what does this prove," said Sister Anne, "but that somebody moved the coffin, and broke the cane?"

"Somebody! *who's somebody?*" said the beadle, staring round about him. And all of a sudden he started back with a tremendous roar, that made the ladies scream and all the glasses on the sideboard jingle, and cried, "*That's the man!*"

He pointed to the portrait of Bluebeard, which stood over the jingling glasses on the sideboard. "That's the man I saw last night walking round the vault, as I'm a living sinner. I saw him a-walking round and round, and, when I went up to speak to him, I'm blessed if he didn't go in at the iron gate, which opened afore him like — like winking, and then in at the vault door, which I'd double-locked, my lady, and bolted inside, I'll take my oath on it!"

"Perhaps you had given him the key?" suggested Sister Anne.

"It's never been out of my pocket. Here it is," cried the beadle; "I'll have no more to do with it." And he flung down the ponderous key, amidst another scream from Widow Bluebeard.

"At what hour did you see him?" gasped she.

"At twelve o'clock, of course."

"It must have been at that very hour," said she, "I heard the voice."

"What voice?" said Anne.

"A voice that called, 'Fatima! Fatima! Fatima!' three times, as plain as ever voice did."

"It didn't speak to me," said the beadle; "it only nodded its head, and wagged its head and beard."

"W—w—was it a *bl—ue beard?*" said the widow.

"Powder-blue, ma'am, as I've a soul to save!"

Dr. Drench was of course instantly sent for. But what are the medicaments of the apothecary in a case where the grave gives up its dead? Dr. Sly arrived, and he offered ghostly — ah! too ghostly — consolation. He said he believed in them. His own grandmother had appeared to his grandfather several times before he married again. He could not doubt that supernatural agencies were possible, even frequent.

"Suppose he were to appear to me alone," ejaculated the widow, "I should die of fright."

The doctor looked particularly arch. "The best way

in these cases, my dear madam," said he, "the best way for unprotected ladies is to get a husband. I never heard of a first husband's ghost appearing to a woman and her second husband in my life. In all history there is no account of one."

"Ah! why should I be afraid of seeing my Bluebeard again?" said the widow; and the doctor retired quite pleased, for the lady was evidently thinking of a second husband.

"The captain would be a better protector for me certainly than Mr. Sly," thought the lady, with a sigh; "but Mr. Sly will certainly kill himself, and will the captain be a match for two ghosts? Sly will kill himself; but ah! the captain won't." And the widow thought with pangs of bitter mortification of Dolly Coddlins. How — how should these distracting circumstances be brought to an end?

She retired to rest that night not without a tremor, — to bed, but not to sleep. At midnight a voice was heard in her room, crying, "Fatima! Fatima! Fatima!" in awful accents. The doors banged to and fro, the bells began to ring, the maids went up and down stairs skurrying and screaming, and gave warning in a body. John Thomas, as pale as death, declared that he found Bluebeard's yeomanry sword, that hung in the hall, drawn, and on the ground; and the sticking-plaster miniature in Mr. Bluebeard's bedroom was found turned topsy-turvy!

"It is some trick," said the obstinate and incredulous Sister Anne. "To-night I will come and sleep with you, sister." And the night came, and the two sisters retired together.

'T was a wild night. The wind howling without went crashing through the old trees of the old rookery round about the old church. The long bedroom windows went thump thumping; the moon could be seen through them lighting up the graves with their ghastly shadows; the yew-tree, cut into the shape of a bird, looked particularly dreadful, and bent and swayed as if it would peck something off that other yew-tree which was of the shape of a dumb-waiter. The bells at midnight began to ring as usual, the doors clapped, jingle — jingle down came a suit of armor in the hall, and a voice came and cried, "Fatima! Fatima! Fatima! look, look, look; the tomb, the tomb, the tomb!"

She looked. The vault door was open, and there in the moonlight stood Bluebeard, exactly as he was represented in the picture, in his yeomanry dress, his face frightfully pale, and his great blue beard curling over his chest, as awful as Mr. Muntz's.

Sister Anne saw the vision as well as Fatima. We shall spare the account of their terrors and screams. Strange to say, John Thomas, who slept in the attic above his mistress's bedroom, declared he was on the watch all night, and had seen nothing in the churchyard, and heard no sort of voices in the house.

And now the question came, What could the ghost want by appearing? "Is there anything," exclaimed the unhappy and perplexed Fatima, "that he would have me do? It is well to say 'now, now, now,' and to show himself; but what is it that makes my blessed husband so uneasy in his grave?" And all parties consulted agreed that it was a very sensible question.

John Thomas, the footman, whose excessive terror at the appearance of the ghost had procured him his mistress's confidence, advised Mr. Screw, the butler, who communicated with Mrs. Baggs, the housekeeper, who condescended to impart her observations to Mrs. Bustle, the lady's-maid, — John Thomas, I say, decidedly advised that my lady should consult a cunning man. There was such a man in town; he had prophesied who should marry his (John Thomas's) cousin; he had cured Farmer Horn's cattle, which were evidently bewitched; he could raise ghosts, and make them speak, and he therefore was the very person to be consulted in the present juncture.

"What nonsense is this you have been talking to the maids, John Thomas, about the conjurer who lives in — in —"

"In Hangman's Lane, ma'am, where the gibbet used to stand," replied John, who was bringing in the muffins. "It's no nonsense, my lady. Every word as that man says comes true, and he knows everything."

"I desire you will not frighten the girls in the servants' hall with any of those silly stories," said the widow; and the meaning of this speech may, of course, at once be guessed. It was that the widow meant to consult the conjurer that very night. Sister Anne said that she would never, under such circumstances, desert her dear Fatima. John Thomas was summoned to attend the ladies with a dark lantern, and forth they set on their perilous visit to the conjurer at his dreadful abode in Hangman's Lane.

What took place at that frightful interview has never been entirely known. But there was no disturbance in the house on the night after. The bells slept quite quietly, the doors did not bang in the least, twelve o'clock struck, and no ghost appeared in the churchyard, and the whole family had a quiet night. The widow attributed this to a sprig of rosemary which the wizard gave her, and a horseshoe which she flung into the garden round the family vault, and which would keep *any* ghost quiet.

It happened the next day, that, going to her milliner's, Sister Anne met a gentleman who has been before mentioned in this story, Ensign Trippet by name; and, indeed, if the truth must be known, it somehow happened that she met the ensign somewhere every day of the week.

"What news of the ghost, my dearest Miss Shacabac?" said he (you may guess on what terms the two young people were by the manner in which Mr. Trippet addressed the lady); "has Bluebeard's ghost frightened your sister into any more fits, or set the bells a-ringing?"

Sister Anne, with a very grave air, told him that he must not joke on so awful a subject, that the ghost had been laid for a while, that a cunning man had told her sister things so wonderful that *any* man must believe in them; that among other things, he had shown to Fatima her future husband.

"Had," said the ensign, "he black whiskers and a red coat?"

"No," answered Anne, with a sigh, "he had red whiskers and a black coat."

"It can't be that rascal Sly!" cried the ensign. But Anne only sighed more deeply and would not answer yes or no. "You may tell the poor captain," she said, "there is no hope for him, and all he has left is to hang himself."

"He shall cut the throat of Sly first, though," replied Mr. Trippet, fiercely. But Anne said things were not decided as yet. Fatima was exceedingly restive, and unwilling to acquiesce in the idea of being married to Mr. Sly; she had asked for further authority. The wizard said he could bring her own husband from the grave to point out her second bridegroom, who shall be, can be, must be, no other than Frederick Sly.

"It is a trick," said the ensign; but Anne was too much frightened by the preceding evening's occurrences to say so. "To-night," she said, "the grave will tell all." And she left Ensign Trippet in a very solemn and affecting way.

. . . .

At midnight, three figures were seen to issue from Widow Bluebeard's house, and pass through the churchyard turnstile, and so away among the graves.

"To call up a ghost is bad enough," said the wizard; "to make him speak is awful. I recommend you, ma'am, to beware, for such curiosity has been fatal to many. There was one Arabian necromancer of my acquaintance who tried to make a ghost speak, and was torn in pieces on the spot. There was another person who *did* hear a ghost speak certainly, but came away from the interview deaf and dumb. There was another — "

"Never mind," says Mrs. Bluebeard, all her old curiosity aroused, "see him and hear him I will. Have n't I seen him and heard him, too, already? When he's audible *and* visible, *then*'s the time."

"But when you heard him," said the necromancer, "he was invisible, and when you saw him he was inaudible; so make up your mind what you will ask him, for ghosts will stand no shilly-shallying. I knew a stuttering man who was flung down by a ghost, and —"

"I *have* made up my mind," said Fatima, interrupting him.

"To ask him what husband you shall take," whispered Anne.

Fatima only turned red, and Sister Anne squeezed her hand; they passed into the graveyard in silence.

There was no moon; the night was pitch dark. They threaded their way through the graves, stumbling over them here and there. An owl was toowhooing from the church tower, a dog was howling somewhere, a cock began to crow, as they will sometimes at twelve o'clock at night.

"Make haste," said the wizard. "Decide whether you will go on or not."

"Let us go back, sister," said Anne.

"I *will* go on," said Fatima. "I should die if I gave it up, I feel I should."

"Here's the gate; kneel down," said the wizard. The women knelt down.

"Will you see your first husband or your second husband?"

"I will see Bluebeard first," said the widow; "I shall

know then whether this be a mockery, or you have the power you pretend to."

At this the wizard uttered an incantation, so frightful, and of such incomprehensible words, that it is impossible for any mortal man to repeat them. And at the end of what seemed to be a versicle of his chant he called Bluebeard. There was no noise but the moaning of the wind in the trees, and the toowhooing of the owl in the tower.

At the end of the second verse he paused again, and called *Bluebeard*. The cock began to crow, the dog began to howl, a watchman in the town began to cry out the hour, and there came from the vault within a hollow groan, and a dreadful voice said, "Who wants me?"

Kneeling in front of the tomb, the necromancer began the third verse. As he spoke, the former phenomena were still to be remarked. As he continued, a number of ghosts rose from their graves, and advanced round the kneeling figures in a circle. As he concluded, with a loud bang the door of the vault flew open, and there in blue light stood Bluebeard in his blue uniform, waving his blue sword, and flashing his blue eyes round about!

"Speak now, or you are lost," said the necromancer to Fatima. But, for the first time in her life, she had not a word to say. Sister Anne, too, was dumb with terror. And, as the awful figure advanced towards them as they were kneeling, the sister thought all was over with them, and Fatima once more had occasion to repent her fatal curiosity.

The figure advanced, saying, in dreadful accents, "Fatima! Fatima! Fatima! wherefore am I called from my grave?" when all of a sudden down dropped his sword, down the ghost of Bluebeard went on his knees, and, clasping his hands together, roared out, "Murder, mercy!" as loud as man could roar.

Six other ghosts stood round the kneeling group. "Why do you call me from the tomb?" said the first; "Who dares disturb my grave?" said the second; "Seize him and away with him!" cried the third. "Murder, mercy!" still roared the ghost of Bluebeard, as the white-robed spirits advanced and caught hold of him.

"It's only Tom Trippet," said a voice at Anne's ear.

"And your very humble servant," said a voice well known to Mrs. Bluebeard; and they helped the ladies to rise, while the other ghosts seized Bluebeard. The necromancer took to his heels and got off; he was found to be no other than Mr. Claptrap, the manager of the theatre.

It was some time before the ghost of Bluebeard could recover from the fainting-fit into which he had been plunged when seized by the opposition ghosts in white; and while they were ducking him at the pump his blue beard came off, and he was discovered to be — who do you think? Why, Mr. Sly, to be sure; and it appears that John Thomas, the footman, had lent him the uniform, and had clapped the doors, and rung the bells, and spoken down the chimney; and it was Mr. Claptrap who gave Mr. Sly the blue fire and the theatre gong; and he went to London next morning by the coach; and, as it was discovered that the story concerning Miss Coddlins was a shameful calumny, why, of course, the widow married Captain Blackbeard. Dr. Sly married them, and has always declared that he knew nothing of his nephew's doings, and wondered that he has not tried to commit suicide since his last disappointment.

Mr. and Mrs. Trippet are likewise living happily together, and this, I am given to understand, is the ultimate fate of a family in whom we were all very much interested in early life.

You will say that the story is not probable. Pshaw! Is n't it written in a book? and is it a whit less probable than the first part of the tale?

THE PICNIC PARTY.

BY HORACE SMITH.

TO give a picnic party a fair chance of success, it must be almost impromptu: projected at twelve o'clock at night at the earliest, executed at twelve o'clock on the following day at the latest; and even then the odds are fearfully against it. The climate of England is not remarkable for knowing its own mind; nor is the weather "so fixed in its resolve" but that a bright August moon, suspended in a clear sky, may be lady-usher to a morn of fog, sleet, and drizzle. Then, again, — but this being tender ground, we will only hint at the possibility of such a change, — a lady of the intended party might quit the drawing-room at night in the sweetest humor imaginable, and make her appearance at breakfast in a less amiable mood, or, perhaps, "prefer taking breakfast in her own room," — from which notice husbands sometimes infer that such a change has taken place.

Mr. Claudius Bagshaw, a retired silk mercer, in the vicinity of London, determined, notwithstanding all these arguments, to have a picnic party on the 24th of August, his wedding-day. On the 3d of July, Mr. Claudius Bagshaw, after eating his breakfast and reading the Morning Post, looked out of his parlor window to watch the horticultural pursuits of his better part. Mr. Bagshaw had become a member of one of the "march-of-intellect-societies," and was confident that the picnic would turn out a very pleasant thing.

"How fortunate we shall be, dear," said Mr. Bagshaw, "how happy we shall be, if the weather should be as fine on our wedding-day as it is now."

"True, love," replied Mrs. Bagshaw; "but this is only the 3d of July, and, as the anniversary of our happy day is the 24th of August, the weather *may* change."

This proposition Mr. Bagshaw did not attempt to deny.

The Bagshaws were the happiest couple in the world. Being blessed with the negative blessing of no offspring, the stream of their affections was not diverted into little channels, but ebbed and flowed in one uninterrupted tide reciprocally from bosom to bosom. They never disputed, they never quarrelled. Yes, they did sometimes, but then it was from a mutual over-anxiety to please. Each was afraid to pronounce a choice, or a preference, lest it might be disagreeable to the other; and hence there occasionally did arise little bickerings, and tiffings, and miffings, which were quite as unpleasant in their effects, and sometimes as difficult to settle, as quarrels originating in less amiable causes.

"But," said Mr. Bagshaw, referring to the barometer, "the instrument for indicating the present state and probable changes of the weather still maintains its elevation, and I tell you what, dear, if the weather should be *preposterous* on the 24th of August, suppose, instead of going into the north, as we did last year, we migrate into Kent or Surrey? Instead of dining at Hampstead, as we did last year, shall we go to Greenwich, or to Putney, and eat little fishes?"

"Whichever you like, love," was the lady's answer to the so-intended question.

"But I put it to your choice, dear."

"Either — or neither — please yourself, love, and you are sure you will please me."

"Pshaw! but it is for the gratification of your — or, more properly speaking, for your gratification. I submit to you an alternative for the purpose of election; and you know, Jane, I repudiate indifference, even as concerning or applying to trifles."

"You know, Claudius, we have but one wish, and that is to please each other; so do you decide."

"But, Mrs. Bagshaw, I must promulgate a request that — having, as I have, no desire but to please you — you will — "

"How, sir! would you force me to choose, when I am so obedient as to choose that you should have the choice entirely your own way? This treatment of me is monstrous!"

And here Mrs. Bagshaw did what is usual and proper for ladies to do on such occasions, — she burst into tears.

"Why, then, madam, to use a strong expression, I must say that — "

But a loud rap at the street-door prevented the utterance of an "expression," the force of which would doubtless have humbled Mrs. Claudius Bagshaw down to the very dust.

"Claudius," said the lady, hastily drying her eyes, "that is Uncle John's knock. We'll go to Gre — Put — Greenwich, love."

"That's well, dear; and be assured, love, that nothing is so adverse to the constitution of what Locke emphatically calls the human mind, philosophically considered, as to persevere in that state of indecision which — that — whereof — but we will not go to either; Uncle John shall select the locality."

Uncle John was a bachelor of fifty-five, possessing twelve thousand pounds, a strong disinclination to part with any of them, a good heart, and a bad temper.

"Good morning t' ye, good folks; as usual, I perceive, billing and cooing."

The Bagshaws had by this time got together in a corner of the garden, and were lovingly occupied in trimming the same pot of sweet peas.

"Quite the contrary, Uncle John," said Mrs. Bagshaw. "Claudius and I have just had one of our most desperate quarrels."

And here the happy pair giggled, and exchanged looks which were meant to imply that *their* most desperate quarrels were mere kitten's play; and that Uncle John did so interpret them, he made manifest by a knowing shake of his forefinger.

"The fact is, sir, Jane and I talk of commemorating the annual recurrence of the anniversary of our wedding-day, at some place a *leetle* farther in the country; but our minds are in a perfect vacuum concerning the identity of the spot. Now, sir, will you reduce the place to a mathematical certainty, and be one of the party?"

"Why — um — no; these things are expensive; we come home at night with a guinea apiece less in our pockets, and I don't see the good of that."

"I have it!" cried Bagshaw; "we'll make it a picnic; that *won't* be expensive."

"Then I'm with you, Bagshaw, with all my heart, — and it shall be *al fresco*."

"There or anywhere else you please, sir," gravely replied the learned member of the universal-knowledge-warehouse.

"Uncle John means in the open air, Claudius; that *will* be delightful."

"Charming!" rejoined Bagshaw.

It may be inquired why Uncle John, who objected to the disbursement of a guinea for a day's pleasure, should so readily have yielded at the suggestion of a picnic. Uncle John possessed a neat little morocco pocket-case, containing a dozen silver spoons, and silver-handled knives and forks, and although we are told that these implements are of later invention than fingers, there is, nevertheless, a very general bias in their favor, for the purpose to which they are applied. Now, Uncle John being aware of the prevalence of their employment, it was for this reason he never objected to make one of a picnic party; for, whilst others contributed chickens, pigeon-pies, or wines, — it being the principle of such parties that each member should furnish something to the feast,—Uncle John invariably contributed the use of his knives, forks, and spoons.

The whole morning was spent in debating on who should be invited to partake of this "pleasantest thing that ever was," and examining into their several pretensions, and their powers of contributing to the amusements of the day; when, at length, the honor of nomination was conferred upon the persons following, and for the reasons assigned:—

Sir Thomas and Lady Grouts—because of their title, which would give an air to the thing—(Sir Thomas, formerly a corn-chandler, having been knighted for carrying up an address in the late reign). Miss Euphemia Grouts, daughter No. 1—who would bring her guitar. Miss Corinna Grouts, ditto No. 2—because she would sing.

Mr. and Mrs. Snodgrass—Mr. Snodgrass being vice-president of the grand junction march-of-intellect society. Mr. Frederick Snodgrass, their son (lately called to the chancery bar), who would bring his flute.

Messrs. Wrench and son (eminent dentists). The father to be invited because he was charming company, and the son, a dead bore, because the father would be offended if he were not. And, lastly,

Miss Snubbleston, a rich maiden lady of forty-four, for no other earthly qualification whatever than her carriage, which (to use Bagshaw's words) would carry herself and *us three*, and also transplant a large portion of the provender to the place of rendezvous.

Bagshaw having made out a fair copy of this list, somewhat in the shape of a bill of parcels, this, the first step towards the "pleasantest thing that ever was," was taken with entire satisfaction.

"Why, Bagshaw," exclaimed Uncle John, who had cast up the numbers, "including our three selves, we shall be thirteen!"

The member of the institution perceived the cause of his alarm! but having been lectured out of *prejudices* respecting matters of greater moment than this, he prepared a look of ineffable contempt as his only reply; however, happening to think of Uncle John's twelve thousand pounds, he suppressed it, and just contented himself with,

"And what then, sir?"

"Why, *then*, sir, that is a risk I won't run; and unless we can manage to — I have it! the very man. How came we to forget him? *The — very — man!* You know Jack Richards?"

The last four words were delivered in a tone implying the utter impossibility of any human creature being unacquainted with Jack Richards.

"Not in the least, sir. I never heard of him."

"What! never heard of Ja — The thing is impossible; everybody knows Jack Richards. The very thing for us; such a wit! such a wag! — he is the life and soul of everything. Should he be unengaged for the 24th of August. But he is so caught up! I was invited to meet him at dinner last Sunday at Jones's, but he did n't come. Such a disappointment to us! However, I shall meet him on Thursday at the Tims's, if he should but keep his promise, and then —"

"But, uncle," said Mrs. Bagshaw, "had n't you better send him an invitation at once?"

"I'll do better still, my dear; I'll call at his lodgings, and if I find him hanging loose, I'll bring him to dine with you to-day." Then, turning to Bagshaw, he added, "That a man like *you* should n't know Jack Richards, is surprising!"

As this was evidently pointed at Mr. Claudius Bagshaw in his capacity of member of a learned body, Bagshaw pursed up his mouth into a mock-modesty smile, and slightly bowed. Off went Uncle John in quest of Jack Richards; and, that the pleasantest thing in the world might not suffer by delay, off went Mr. Bagshaw to apprize the Snodgrasses, the Groutses, and the rest of the nominees; and, more important still, off went the lady to the poulterer's, to inquire whether he was likely to have any nice pigeons for a pie, about the twenty-third of next month. The dinner-hour arrived, and so did Uncle John, but with a face of unspeakable woe.

"I feared how it would be."

"What! can't he be with us on the 24th?" inquired both the Bagshaws at the same instant.

"He will if he can; but he won't promise. But to-day! — However, it serves us right; we were unwise to indulge a hope of his coming at so short a notice. He has almost engaged himself to you for Sunday fortnight, though. What a creature it is! — he has given me such a pain in my side!"

"Something he said that almost killed you with laughing? Repeat it, uncle, repeat it."

"Why, no, he did n't say anything particular; but he has a knack of poking one in the ribs, in his comical way, and sometimes he hurts you."

We intended to describe Jack Richards at length; Uncle John's accidental notice of this trait has, most probably, rendered that trouble unnecessary. Indeed, we feel that we need scarcely add to it, that he can sing a devilish good song (and everybody knows what is meant by that), and imitated the inimitable Mathews's imitations of the actors, not even excepting his imitation of Tate Wilkinson's imitation of Garrick.

Except the uncertainty of Jack Richards, the result of the morning's occupation was satisfactory. Bagshaw, still retaining his old business-like habits of activity and industry, had contrived to wait on every person named in the list, all of whom had promised their attendance; and Mrs. Bagshaw had received from the poulterer a positive assurance that he would raise heaven and earth to supply her with pigeons on the 23d of the ensuing August!

Committees were forthwith summoned. First, a committee to consider of the whereabout. At this, after an evening of polite squabbling, which had nearly put an end to the project altogether, Twickenham meadows received the honor of selection, — *nem. con.* as Bagshaw said. Next, lest it should happen, as it did once happen, for want of such preconcert, that a picnic party of ten found themselves at their place of meeting with ten fillets of veal and ten hams, Mr. Bagshaw called a committee of "provender." Here it was settled that the Snodgrasses should contribute four chickens and a tongue; the Bagshaws, their pigeon-pie; Wrench and son, a ham; Sir Thomas Grouts, a hamper of his own *choice* wine; Miss Snubbleston, a basket of fruit and pastry;

Uncle John, his silver spoons, knives, and forks; and Jack Richards — his charming company. And lastly came the committee for general purposes! At this important meeting, it was agreed that the party proceed to Twickenham by water; that to save the trouble of loading and unloading, Miss Snubbleston's carriage convey the hampers, etc., direct to the place appointed,— the said carriage, moreover, serving to bring the ladies to town, should the evening prove cold; that, for the *water-music*, the following programme be adopted: 1. On reaching Vauxhall Bridge, the concert to commence with Madame Pasta's grand scena in "Medea," previous to the murder of the children, by Miss Corinna Grouts. 2. Nicholson's grand flute concerto in five sharps, by Mr. Frederick Snodgrass. 3. Grand aria, with variations, guitar, by Miss Euphemia Grouts. 4. Sweet Bird; accompaniment, flute obligato, Miss C. G. and Mr. F. S. — and 5. The Dettingen Te Deum (arranged for three voices, by Mr. F. S.) by Miss Euphemia, Miss Corinna, and Mr. Frederick Snodgrass. The "interstices," as Mr. Bagshaw called them, to be filled up by the amusing talents of the elder Wrench and Uncle John's friend. And, lastly, that the company do assemble at Mr. Bagshaw's on the morning of the 24th of August, at ten o'clock *precisely*, in order to have the advantage of the tide both ways.

Three days prior to the important 24th, Mr. Bagshaw went to engage the boat, but, in a squabble with the boatman, Mr. B. got a black eye. This was the first mishap.

Restless and impatient though you be, depend upon

it, there is not a day of the whole three hundred and sixty-five will put itself, in the slightest degree, out of the way, or appear one second before its appointed time, for your gratification. O that people would consider this, and await events with patience! Certainly Mr. Bagshaw did not. The night of the 23d to him appeared an age. His repeater was in his hand every ten minutes. He thought the morning would never dawn, — but he was mistaken; it did; and as fine a morning as if it had been made on purpose to favor his excursion. By six o'clock he was dressed! — by eight the contributions from all the members had arrived, and were ranged in the passage. There was their own pigeon-pie, carefully packed in brown paper and straw; Sir Thomas's hamper of his own choice wine; and the rest. Everything promised fairly. The young ladies and Mr. Frederick had had thirty rehearsals of their grand arias and concertos, and were perfect to a demi-semiquaver; Jack Richards would *certainly* come; and the only drawback upon Mr. Bagshaw's personal enjoyment — but nothing in this world is perfect — was the necessity he was under of wearing his green shade, which would totally deprive him of the pleasure of contemplating the beauties of the Thames scenery, — a thing he had set his heart upon. Nine! ten!

"No one here yet! Jane, my love, we shall infallibly lose the tide." And for the next quarter of an hour the place of the poor repeater was no sinecure.

A knock! Mr. and Mrs. Snodgrass and Mr. Frederick. Another! The whole family of the Groutses. Next came Mr. Charles Wrench.

"Bless us! Mr. Charles," said Bagshaw, "where is your father?"

Now, Mr. Wrench, senior, was an agreeable old dentist, always gay, generally humorous, sometimes witty; he could *sketch* characters as well as *draw* teeth; and, on occasions of this kind, was invaluable. The son was a mere donkey; a silly, simpering, well-dressed young gentleman, the owner of no more than the eighth of an idea, and of a very fine set of teeth, which he constantly exhibited like a sign or advertisement of his shop. Appended to everything he uttered were a preface and postscript, in the form of a sort of Billy-goat grin.

"He! he! he! he! Fayther regrets emezingly he caint come, being called to attend the Duchess of Dilborough. He! he! he! he!"

As we have already said that it was in pure compliment to the father that the son was invited, and not at all for the sake of his own company, his presence was a grievous aggravation of the disappointment.

The next knock announced Miss Snubbleston. But where was her carriage? Why, it had been newly varnished, and they might scratch her panels with the hampers; and then she was afraid of her springs. So here was Miss Snubbleston without her carriage, for the convenience of which alone she had been invited, considered by the rest in exactly the same light as young Mr. Wrench without old Mr. Wrench, — *id est*, a damper. A new arrangement was the necessary consequence; and the baskets, under the superintendence of a servant, were jolted down in a hackney-coach, to be embarked at Westminster. But Miss Snubbleston brought with her a substitute, which was by no means a compensation. Cupid, her wretched, little, barking, yelping, Dutch pug, had eaten something that had disagreed with him, and his fair mistress would not "for worlds" have left him at home while he was so indisposed. Well, no one chose to be the first to object to the intruder, so Cupid was received.

"But where can Uncle John and his friend be? We shall lose the tide, that's certain," was scarcely uttered by Mr. Bagshaw, when in came our uncle, together with the long-expected Jack Richards.

The usual introductions over, Mr. Richards saluted everybody with the self-sufficient swagger of a vulgar lion.

"The day smiles auspicious, sir," said Bagshaw, who thought it requisite he should throw off something fine to so celebrated a person.

"Smile? — a broad grin, I call it, sir." And here was a general laugh.

"O, excellent!"

"Capital!"

Uncle John, proud of his friend, whispered in Bagshaw's ear, "You see, Jack's beginning." And now hats and gloves were in motion.

"You have got your flute, Frederick?"

"Yes, mother," was the reply.

"Lau, ma," cried Miss Corinna, "if I haven't come without 'Sweet Bird,' and my scena from 'Medea,' I declare."

As these were indispensable to the amusements of the day, a servant was despatched for them. He couldn't be gone longer than half an hour. Half an hour! thought Bagshaw; 'tis eleven now; and the tide. — But the servant was absent a few minutes beyond the half-hour, and poor Bagshaw suffered severely from that gnawing impatience, amounting almost to pain, which every mother's son of us has experienced upon occasions of greater — or less importance than this. They were again at the very point of starting, when a message was brought to Mrs. Snodgrass that little Master Charles had cut his thumb dreadfully! What was to be done? Mrs. Snodgrass vowed she should n't be easy in her mind the whole day unless she knew the extent of the mischief; and as they *only* lived in Euston Square, and she could be there and back again in twenty minutes, she would herself go see what really was the matter, — and away she went. Twenty minutes! During all this time, Bagshaw — but who would attempt to describe anguish indescribable? At length he was relieved by the return of Mrs. Snodgrass; but, to the horror and consternation of himself and of all present, she introduced the aforesaid Master Charles, — an ugly, ill-tempered, blubbering little brat of seven years old, with a bloated red face, scrubby white hair, and red eyes; and with the interesting appendage of a thick slice of bread and butter in his hand.

"I'm sure you'll pardon this liberty," said the affectionate mamma; "but poor Charley has cut himself very much, and he would not be pacified till I consented to take him with us. He has promised to be very good. There, don't cry any more, darling!" and, accordingly, the urchin roared with tenfold vigor. There were no particular manifestations of joy at this arrival; and it is just possible, although nothing was uttered to that effect, that there did exist a general and cordial wish that young Master Snodgrass were sprawling at the bottom of the deepest well in England. Uncle John, indeed, did utter something about the pug and the child — two such nuisances — people bringing their brats into grown-up company.

At length the procession set out: the Bagshaws, Uncle John, and Jack Richards bringing up the rear in a hackney-coach. On reaching the corner of the street, Mrs. Bagshaw called out to the driver to stop.

"What is the matter, dear?" said Bagshaw.

"Your eye-lotion, love."

"Well, never mind that, sweet."

"Claudius, I shall be miserable if you go without it. Dr. Nooth desired you would use it every two hours. I must insist, — now, for my sake, love, — such an eye as he has got, Mr. Richards!"

So away went Bagshaw to the Lake of Lausanne Lodge for the lotion, which, as it always happens when folks are in a hurry, it took him a quarter of an hour to find.

They were now fairly on the road.

"What a smell of garlic!" exclaimed Uncle John; "it is intolerable!"

"Dear me!" said Mr. Richards, "do you perceive it? 'T is a fine Italian sausage I bought at Morel's, as my contribution. We shall find it an excellent relish in the country." And he exhibited his purchase, enveloped in a brown paper.

"Pha! shocking!—'t is a perfect nuisance! Put it into your pocket again, or throw it out at the window." But Mr. Richards preferred obeying the first command.

Apropos of contributions —"Uncle, have you brought your spoons?"

"Here they are," replied Uncle, at the same time drawing from his pocket a parcel in size and form very closely resembling Mr. Richards's offensive contribution.

On arriving at Westminster Bridge, they found the rest of the party already seated in the barge, and the first sound that saluted their ears was an intimation that, owing to their being two hours behind time (it was now past twelve), they should hardly save the tide.

"I knew it would be so," said Bagshaw, with more of discontent than he had thought to experience, considering the pains he had taken that everything should be well ordered.

As Uncle John was stepping into the boat, Richards, with great dexterity, exchanged parcels with him, putting the Italian sausage into Uncle John's pocket and the spoons into his own; enhancing the wit of the manœuvre by whispering to the Bagshaws, who, with infinite delight, had observed it.

"Hang me," said Richards, "but he shall have enough of the garlic!"

The old gentleman was quite unconscious of the operation, as Richards adroitly diverted his attention from it by giving him one of his facetious pokes in the ribs, which nearly bent him double, and drew a roar of laughter from every one else.

Just as they were pushing off, their attention was attracted by a loud howling. It proceeded from a large Newfoundland dog which was standing at the water's edge.

"Confound it!" cried Richards, "that's my Carlo! He has followed me, unperceived, all the way from home — I would not lose him for fifty pounds. I must take him back — pray put me ashore. This is very provoking — though he is *a very quiet dog!*"

There was no mistaking this hint. Already were there two nuisances on board, — Master Charles and the Dutch pug: but as they were to choose between Jack Richards with his dog, or no Jack Richards (or in other words, no life and soul of the party), it was presently decided that Carlo should be invited to a seat on the hampers, which were stowed at the head of the boat, — Uncle John having first extracted from Mr. Richards an assurance that their new guest would lie there as still as a mouse. This complaisance was amply rewarded by a speedy display of Mr. Richards's powers of entertainment. As soon as they reached the middle of the river Jack Richards suddenly jumped up, for the purpose of frightening Miss Snubbleston; a jest at which everybody else would have laughed, had not their own lives been endangered by it. Even his great admirer suggested to him that once of that was enough. His next joke was one of a more intellectual character. Though he had never till this day seen Sir Thomas, he had accidentally heard something about his former trade.

"What is the difference between Lord Eldon and Sir Thomas Grouts?" Nobody could tell.

"One is an ex-chancellor, — the other is an ex-chandler." Everybody laughed, except the Grouts family.

This was succeeded by another thrust in Uncle John's side; after which came a pun, which we shall not record, as the effect of it was to force the ladies to cough and look into the water, the gentlemen to look at each other, and Mrs. Snodgrass to whisper to Mrs. Bagshaw, —

"Who *is* this Mr. Richards?"

Indeed, there would have been no end to his pleasantries had they not been interrupted by a request that Miss Corinna would open the concert, as they were fast approaching Vauxhall Bridge. Mr. Bagshaw (looking at the programme, which he had drawn out on paper ruled with red and blue lines) objected to this, as it would disturb the previous arrangement, according to which the concert was not to commence till they were *through* the bridge. This objection was overruled, and the fair Corinna unrolled the music, for which the servant had been despatched with so much haste. Miss Corinna screamed. What was the matter?

"They had not sent the grand scena from Medea, after all, but a wrong piece!" And the pains she had taken to be perfect in it!

"Could not Miss Corinna sing it from memory?"

"Impossible!"

"How careless of you, Corinna! then sing what they have sent."

"Why, ma," said Corinna, with tears in her eyes, and holding up the unfortunate sheets, — "why, bless me, ma, I can't sing the overture to Der Freyschutz!"

The difficulty of such a performance being readily admitted, Mr. Frederick Snodgrass declared himself but too happy to comply with the calls for his concerto in five sharps, which stood next on the list; and with the air of one well satisfied that an abundance of admiration and applause would reward his efforts, he drew forth his flute, when, lo! one of the joints was missing! This accident was nearly fatal to the musical entertainments of the day; for not only was the concerto thereby rendered impracticable, but "Sweet Bird" with the flute-accompaniment obligato, was put *hors de combat*. Disappointment having, by this, been carried to its uttermost bounds, the announcement that two strings of the guitar had gone was received with an indifference almost stoical; and every one was grateful to Miss Euphemia for so *willingly* undertaking (the whispered menaces of Lady Grouts being heard by nobody but the young lady herself) to do all that could be done under such untoward circumstances. She would endeavor to accompany herself through a little ballad; but she failed.

Mr. Claudius Bagshaw, with all his literature, science, and philosophy, now, for the first time, wondered how anything could fail, so much trouble having been taken to insure success. Drawing forth his repeater, he ahem'd, and just muttered,—

"Unaccountable! Hem! upon my word! One o'clock, and no pleasure yet!"

"One o'clock!" echoed his spouse; "then 't is time for your eye, dear!" And Bagshaw was compelled not only to suffer his damaged optics to be dabbled by his tormentingly affectionate wife, but to submit again to be hoodwinked, in spite of his entreaties to the contrary, and his pathetic assurances that he had not yet seen a bit of the prospect; a thing he had set his heart upon.

Now occurred a dead silence of some minutes. A steamboat rushed by. Bagshaw seized this opportunity to make a display of his scientific acquirements; and this he did with the greater avidity, as he had long wished to astonish Vice-President Snodgrass. Besides, in the event of his offering to deliver a course of lectures at the institution, the vice-president might bear evidence to his capabilities for the purpose, — his acquaintance not only with the facts, but with the terms of science. Whether those terms were always correctly applied, we confess ourselves not sufficiently learned to pronounce.

"How wondrous is the science of mechanism! how variegated its progeny, how simple, yet how compound! I am propelled to the consideration of this subject by having optically perceived that ingenious nautical instrument, which has just now flown along like a mammoth, that monster of the deep! You ask me how are steamboats propagated? in other words, how is such an infinite and immovable body inveigled along its course? I will explain it to you. It is by the power of friction: that is to say, the two wheels, or paddles, turning diametrically, or at the same moment, on the axioms, and repressing by the rotundity of their motion the action of the menstruum in which the machine floats, — water being, in a philosophical sense, a powerful non-conductor, — it is clear, that in proportion as is the revulsion so is the progression; and as is the centrifugal force, so is the —"

"Pooh!" cried Uncle John, impatiently; "let us have some music."

"I have an apprehension, Bagshaw," said the vice-president, — "that I should not presume to dispute with you, — that you are wrong in your theory of the centrifugal force of the axioms. However, we will discuss that point at the grand-junction. But come, Frederick, the 'Dettingen Te Deum.'"

Frederick and the young ladies having, by many rehearsals, perfected themselves in the performance of this piece, instantly complied. Scarcely had they reached the fourth bar, when Jack Richards, who had not for a long time perpetrated a joke, produced a harsh, brassy-toned, German colina, and "blew a blast so loud and shrill," that the Dutch pug began to bark, Carlo to howl, and the other nuisance, Master Charles, to cry. The German colina was of itself bad enough, but these congregated noises were intolerable. Uncle John aimed a desperate blow with a large apple, which he was just about to bite, at the head of Carlo, who, in order to give his lungs fair play, was standing on all fours on the hampers. The apple missed the dog, and went some distance beyond him into the water. Mr. Carlo, attributing to Uncle John a kinder feeling than that which actually prompted the proceeding, looked upon it as a good-natured expedient to afford him an opportunity of adding his mite to the amusements of the day, by displaying a specimen of his training. Without waiting for a second hit, he plunged into the river, seized the apple, and, paddling up the side of the boat with the prize triumphantly exhibited in his jaws, to the consternation of the whole party, he scrambled in between Uncle John and his master, dropped the apple upon the floor, distributed a copious supply of Thames water amongst the affrighted beholders, squeezed his way through them as best he could, and, with an air of infinite self-satisfaction, resumed his place on the hampers.

Had Mr. Jack Richards, the owner of the dog, been at the bottom of the Thames a week before this delightful 24th, not one of the party, Mr. Richards himself excepted, would have felt in the slightest degree concerned; but since, with a common regard to politeness, they could not explicitly tell him so, they contented themselves with bestowing upon Mr. Carlo every term of opprobrium, every form of execration, which good manners will allow, — leaving it to the sagacity of "the life and soul of the company" to apply them to himself, if so it might be agreeable to him. Poor fellow! he felt the awkwardness of his situation, and figuratively, as well as literally speaking, this exploit of his dog threw a *damp* upon him, as it had done upon every one else.

For some time the picnickers pursued their way in solemn silence. At length Bagshaw, perceiving that there would be very little pleasure if matters were allowed to go on in this way, exclaimed, —

"An intelligent observer, not imbued with the knowledge of our intentions, would indicate us to be a combination of perturbed spirits, rowed by Charon across the river Tiber."

In cases of this kind, the essential is to break the ice. Conversation was now resumed.

"Ah! ha!" said the vice-president, "Sion-house."

"The residuum of the Northumberlands," said Claudius, "one of the most genealogical and antique families in England."

And here, having put forth so much classical and historical lore, almost in a breath, he marked his own satisfaction by a short, single cough. The vice-president *said* nothing, but he thought to himself, "There is much more in this Bagshaw than I suspected."

Jack Richards was up again.

"Come, what's done can't be helped; but, upon my soul! I am sorry at being the innocent cause of throwing cold water on the party."

"Cold water, indeed! look at me, sir," said Miss Snubbleston, with tears in her eyes, and exhibiting her *ci-devant* shoulder-of-mutton sleeves, which, but half an hour before as stiff and stately as starch could make them, were now hanging loose and flabby about her skinny arms.

"Too bad, Jack," said Uncle John, "to bring that cursed Carlo of yours!"

Carlo, perceiving that he was the subject of conversation, was instantly on his legs, his eye steadily fixed upon Uncle John, evidently expecting a signal for a second plunge. The alarm was general, and every tongue joined in the scream of "Lie down, sir! lie down!"

Uncle John, who had been more than once offended by the odor from his friend's garlic sausage, and who had on each and every such occasion vented an exclamation of disgust, to the great amusement of Mr. Richards (who chuckled with delight to think of the exchange he had secretly effected) here, in the very middle of the stream, resolved to rid himself of the annoyance. Unperceived by any one, he gently drew the parcel from Richards's coat-pocket, and let it drop into the water! Like King Richard's pierced coffin, once in, it soon found the way to the bottom. Uncle John could scarcely restrain his inclination to laugh aloud; however, he contrived to assume an air of indifference, and whistled part of a tune.

Arrived at Twickenham, the boatmen were ordered to pull up to a beautiful meadow, sloping down to the water's edge. There was no time to lose, — they had had no pleasure yet, — so Bagshaw entreated that every one "would put his shoulder to the wheel, and be on the *qui rala.*" In an instant a large heavy hamper was landed, but as, in compliance with Bagshaw's request, every one did something to *help,* a scene of confusion was the consequence, and numerous pieces of crockery were invalided ere the cloth was properly spread, and the dishes, plates, and glasses distributed. But for the feast. Mr. Snodgrass's basket was opened, and out of it were taken four remarkably fine chickens, and a tongue — uncooked! There was but one mode of accounting for this trifling omission. Mr. Snodgrass's Betty was a downright matter-of-fact person, who obeyed orders to the very letter. Having been told, the evening before, to get four fine chickens for roasting, together with a tongue, and to pack them, next morning, in a basket, she did so literally and strictly; but, as she had received no distinct orders to dress them, to have done so she would have deemed an impertinent departure from her instructions.

Well; since people in a high state of civilization, like Mr. Claudius Bagshaw and his friends, cannot eat raw chickens, they did the only thing they could under the circumstances, — they grumbled exceedingly, and put them back again into the basket. This was a serious deduction in the important point of quantity, and Uncle John felt a slight touch of remorse at having thrown, as he thought, his friend's Italian sausage into the Thames. However, there was still provision in the garrison. But the run of luck in events, as at a game of whist, may be against you; and when it is so, be assured that human prudence and foresight — remarkable as even Mrs. Bagshaw's, who bespoke her pigeons seven weeks before she wanted them — avail but little. When the packages were first stowed in the boat, the pigeon-pie was inadvertently placed at the bottom, and everything else, finishing with the large heavy hamper of crockery, with Carlo on that, upon it; so that when it was taken up it appeared a chaotic mass of pie-crust, broken china, pigeons, brown paper, beefsteak, eggs, and straw!

"Now this is enough to provoke a saint!" said Bagshaw; and no one attempting to deny the position, with this salvo for his own character of philosophic patience, he indulged himself in the full expression of his vexation and sorrow. After a minute examination, he declared the pie to be "a complete squash," and that nobody could venture to eat it but at the imminent risk of being choked. As he was about to throw it over the hedge, Miss Snubbleston, seized with an unusual fit of generosity, called out to him, —

"What *are* you doing? Though it is n't fit for us

to eat, it will be quite a treat to the poor watermen. I dare say, poor souls, they don't often get pigeon-pie."

But the good genius of Mr. Carlo prevailed; and the truth of the adage, "'t is an ill wind that blows nobody good," was confirmed in his mind as he found himself busily employed in the ingenious operation of separating pigeon from porcelain. It was, doubtless, extremely ill-bred in one dog not to invite another, and Cupid expressed his sense of the slight by a long-continued yell, which drew down upon him, from the equally disappointed bipeds of the company, sundry wishes, the positive accomplishment of which would not have tended much to his personal happiness. The next basket was opened. Things were not altogether in a desperate state. Mr. Wrench's ham was in perfect order, and that, with Miss Snubbleston's salad, and some bread, and — could it be possible! After so much preparation, and Mr. Bagshaw's committee of "provender" to boot, that no one should have thought of so obvious a requisite as bread! There would not be time to send Mr. Bagshaw to Twickenham town to procure some, for it was getting late, and if they lost the tide, they should be on the water till midnight, and they did not like the appearance of the sky, which was by no means so blue as it had hitherto been. However, the want of bread did not *much* signify; they could make a shift with Miss Snubbleston's biscuits and pound-cakes. But Uncle John did not come out on an excursion of pleasure to make shift; no more did Bagshaw; no more did any of the others. There was nothing else to be done; so where is Miss Snubbleston's basket? And where is Master Charles? gracious! Don't be alarmed, the precious rarity is in no danger. He was soon discovered behind a tree, whither he had dragged the fruit and cakes, and was engaged with all his might and main, in an endeavor, with a piece of stick, to force out an apple. In this attempt, as it was presently seen, the interesting child had cracked a bottle, the contents of which — merely a preparation of oil, vinegar, and mustard for the salad — were quietly dribbling through the poundcakes, biscuits, and fruit. Similar aspirations to those which had lately been so cordially expressed for the Dutch pug were now most devoutly formed in behalf of Master Charles.

"This comes of bringing their plaguy brats with them," said Uncle and Bagshaw.

Whilst this scene was going on, Jack Richards, perceiving that the service of the table was incomplete, bethought him of Uncle John's silver-handled knives and forks and spoons; he felt first in one pocket, and then in the other, then he ran down to search the boat, then he rummaged the baskets.

"Jack, my boy," hallooed Uncle John, "don't trouble yourself, you'll never see *that* again."

"What, sir?"

"I could not bear the smell of it any longer, so I slyly drew it out of your pocket, and dexterously let it fall into the deepest part of the Thames."

And here Uncle John chuckled, and looked about him for applause.

"Bless me, sir! Don't say so — why — bless my heart — you don't know — before we got into the boat,

I put the sausage into your pocket, and your case of cutlery into my own!"

There was a general burst of laughter against Uncle John. He turned as pale as — nay, paler than anything that has ever yet been dragged into the comparison; for an instant he stood stock-still, then thrust his hand into his pocket, drew forth the unfortunate substitute, and at the same time exclaiming D——tion! dashed it violently to the ground. He next buttoned his coat from the bottom to the top, pulled down his cuffs, whispered to his no longer admired Jack Richards, "You shall hear from me, Mr. ——," and saying aloud to Bagshaw, "This comes of your confounded party of pleasure, sir," away he went, and returned to town outside a Twickenham coach; resolving by the way to call out *that* Mr. Richards, and to eject the Bagshaws from the snug corner they held in his last will and testament.

This explosion seemed to have banished pleasure for that day. They were all, more or less, out of humor; and instead of making the best of things, as they had hitherto done, they now made the worst of them. Sir Thomas's hamper of *his choice wine* (which, by the by, he purchased at a cheap shop for the occasion) was opened; and slices of ham were cut with the only knife and fork. Jack Richards tried to be facetious, but it would not do. He gave Bagshaw a poke in the ribs, which was received with a very formal, "Sir, I must beg —" To Mr. Wrench, junior, he said, —

"You have not spoken much to-day — but you have made amends for your silence — d' ye take? — Your *ham* is good, though your *tongue* is not worth much!"

Instead of laughing, Mr. Wrench simpered something about impertinent liberties and satisfaction. On being invited by Sir Thomas to a second glass of his old East India, he said that one was a dose — had rather not double the *Cape;* and at the first glass of champagne, he inquired whether there had been a plentiful supply of gooseberries that year. In short, whether it were that the company knew not how to appreciate his style of wit and pleasantry, or that he was in reality a very disagreeable person, the fact is that — but hold! let us say nothing ill of him; he died last week, at Folkestone, of a surfeit of goose, in the forty-ninth year of his age. For the consolation of such as were amused by him, and regret his loss, be it remembered that there are still to be found many Jack Richards in this world.

As we have said, they now resolved to make the worst of everything; the grass was damp, the gnats were troublesome, Carlo's nose was in everybody's face, Cupid's teeth at everybody's calves, and Master Charles was ill of the many sour apples; it was growing late, and no good could come of sitting longer in the open air. They re-embarked. By the time they reached Putney it was pitch dark, and the tide was setting against them. They moved on in mute impatience, for there was a slight sprinkling of rain. It now fell in torrents. Master Charles grew frightened and screamed. Cupid yelped, and Carlo howled. Accompanied the rest of the way by these pleasing sounds, at one in the morning (two hours and a half later than they intended) they arrived at Westminster stairs, dull, dreary, drowsy, discontented, and drenched.

FATHER TOM AND THE POPE,

As related by Mr. Michael Heffernan, Master of the National
School at Tallymactaggart, in the County Leitrim, to
a friend, during his official visit to Dublin for
the purpose of studying political econ-
omy, in the spring of 1838.

BY SAMUEL FERGUSON.

I.

HOW FATHER TOM WENT TO TAKE POT-LUCK AT THE VATICAN.

WHEN his Riv'rence was in Room, ov coorse the Pope axed him to take pot-look wid him. More be token, it was on a Friday; but, for all that, there was plenty of mate; for the Pope gev himself an absolution from the fast on account of the great company that was in it, — at laste so I'm tould. Howandiver, there's no fast on the dhrink, anyhow, — glory be to God! — and so, as they wor sitting, afther dinner, taking their sup together, says the Pope, says he, "Thomaus," for the Pope, you know, spakes that away, and all as one as ov uz, — "Thomaus *a lanna*," says he, "I'm tould you welt them English heretics out ov the face."

"You may say that," says his Riv'rence to him again. "Be my soul," says he, "if I put your Holiness undher the table, you won't be the first Pope I floored."

Well, his Holiness laughed like to split; for you know, Pope was the great Prodesan that Father Tom put down upon Purgathory; and ov coorse they knew all the ins and outs of the conthravarsy at Room. "Faix, Thomaus," says he, smiling across the table at him mighty agreeable, — "it's no lie what they tell me, that yourself is the pleasant man over the dhrop ov good liquor."

"Would you like to thry?" says his Riv'rence.

"Sure, and am n't I thrying all I can?" says the Pope. "Sorra betther bottle ov wine's betuxt this and Salamanca, nor there's fornenst you on the table; it's raal Lachrymachrystal, every spudh ov it."

"It's mortial could," says Father Tom.

"Well, man alive," says the Pope, "sure, and here's the best ov good claret in the cut decanther."

"Not maining to make little ov the claret, your Holiness," says his Riv'rence, "I would prefir some hot wather and sugar, wid a glass ov spirits through it, if convanient."

"Hand me over the bottle of brandy," says the Pope to his head butler, "and fetch up the materi'ls," says he.

"Ah, then, your Holiness," says his Riv'rence, mighty eager, "maybe you'd have a dhrop ov the native in your cellar? Sure, it's all one throuble," says he, "and, troth, I dunna how it is, but brandy always plays the puck wid my inthrails."

"'Pon my conscience, then," says the Pope, "it's

very sorry I am, Misther Maguire," says he, "that it is n't in my power to plase you; for I 'm sure and certaint that there 's not as much whiskey in Room this blessed minit as 'ud blind the eye ov a midge."

"Well, in troth, your Holiness," says Father Tom, "I knewn there was no use in axing; only," says he, "I did n't know how else to exqueeze the liberty I tuck," says he, "of bringing a small taste," says he, "of the real stuff," says he, hauling out an imperi'l quart bottle out ov his coat-pocket; "that never seen the face ov a guager," says he, setting it down on the table fornenst the Pope; "and if you 'll jist thry the full ov a thimble ov it, and it does n't rise the cockles ov your Holiness's heart, why then, my name," says he, "is n't Tom Maguire!" and with that he out's wid the cork.

Well, the Pope at first was going to get vexed at Father Tom for fetching dhrink thataway in his pocket, as if there was n't lashins in the house: so says he, "Misther Maguire," says he, "I 'd have you to comprehind the differ betuxt an inwitation to dinner from the succissor of Saint Pether, and from a common mayur or a Prodesan squirean that maybe has n't liquor enough in his cupboard to wet more nor his own heretical whistle. That may be the way wid them that you wisit in Leithrim," says he, "and in Roscommon; and I 'd let you know the differ in the prisint case," says he, "only that you 're a champion ov the Church and entitled to laniency. So," says he, "as the liquor 's come, let it stay. And, in troth, I 'm curi's myself," says he, getting mighty soft when he found the delightful smell ov the *putteen*, "in inwistigating the composition ov distilled liquors; it's a branch ov natural philosophy," says he, taking up the bottle and putting it to his blessed nose.

Ah! my dear, the very first snuff he got ov it, he cried out, the dear man, "Blessed Vargin, but it has the divine smell!" and crossed himself and the bottle half a dozen times running.

"Well, sure enough, it's the blessed liquor now," says his Riv'rence, "and so there can be no harm any way in mixing a dandy of punch; and," says he, stirring up the materi'ls wid his goolden meeddlar, — for everything at the Pope's table, to the very shcrew for drawing the corks, was ov vergin goold, — "if I might make boold," says he, "to spake on so deep a subjic afore your Holiness, I think it 'ud considherably whacilitate the inwestigation ov its chemisthry and phwarmaceutics, if you 'd jist thry the laste sup in life ov it inwardly."

"Well, then, suppose I do make the same expiriment," says the Pope, in a much more condescinding way nor you 'd have expected, — and wid that he mixes himself a real stiff facer.

"Now, your Holiness," says Father Tom, "this bein' the first time you ever dispinsed them chymicals," says he, "I 'll jist make bould to lay doun one rule ov orthography," says he, "for conwhounding them, *secundum mortem*."

"What's that?" says the Pope.

"Put in the spcrits first," says his Riv'rence; "and then put in the sugar; and remember, every dhrop ov wather you put in after that, spoils the punch."

"Glory be to God!" says the Pope, not minding a word Father Tom was saying. "Glory be to God!" says he, smacking his lips. "I never knewn what dhrink was afore," says he. "It bates the Lachymalchrystal out ov the face!" says he, — "it's Necthar itself, it is, so it is!" says he, wiping his epistolical mouth wid the cuff ov his coat.

"'Pon my secret honor," says his Riv'rence, "I'm raally glad to see your Holiness set so much to your satiswhaction; especially," says he, "as, for fear ov accidents, I tuck the liberty of fetching the fellow ov that small vesshel," says he, "in my other coat-pocket. So devil a fear of our running dhry till the but-end of the evening, anyhow," says he.

"Dhraw your stool into the fire, Misther Maguire," says the Pope, "for faix," says he, "I'm bent on anilizing the metaphwysics ov this phinomenon. Come, man alive, clear off," says he, "you're not dhrinking at all."

"Is it dhrink?" says his Riv'rence; "by Gorra, your Holiness," says he, "I'd dhrink wid you till the cows 'ud be coming home in the morning."

So wid that they tackled to, to the second fugil apiece, and fell into a larned discourse.

But it's time for me now to be off to the lecthir at the Boord. O, my sorra light upon you, Docther Whately, wid your plitical econimy and your hydherastatics! What the *divul* use has a poor hedge-masther like me wid sich deep larning as is only fit for the likes ov them two I left over their second tumbler? Howandiver, wishing I was like them, in regard ov the sup ov dhrink, anyhow, I must brake off my norration for the prisint; but when I see you again, I'll tell you how Father Tom made a hare ov the Pope that evening, both in theology and the cube root.

II.

HOW FATHER TOM SACKED HIS HOLINESS IN THEOLOGY AND LOGIC.

WELL, the lecther's over, and I'm kilt out and out. My bitther curse be upon the man that invinted the same Boord! I thought onc't I'd fadomed the say ov throuble; and that was when I got through fractions at ould Mat Kavanagh's school, in Firdramore, — God be good to poor Mat's sowl, though he did deny the cause the day he suffered! but its fluxions itself we're set to bottom now, sink or shwim! May I never die if my head isn't as throughother, as anything wid their ordinals and cardinals, — and, begad, it's all nothing to the econimy lecthir that I have to go to at two o'clock. Howandiver, I mustn't forget that we left his Riv'rence and his Holiness sitting fornenst one another in the parlor ov the Vatican, jist afther mixing their second tumbler.

When they had got well down into the same, they fell, as I was telling you, into learned discourse. For you see, the Pope was curious to find out whether Father Tom was the great theologinall that people said; and says he "Mister Maguire," says he, "What answer do you make to the heretics when they quote them passidges agin thransubstantiation out ov the Fathers?" says he.

"Why," says his Riv'rence, "as there is no sich passidges I make myself mighty asy about them; but if you want to know how I dispose ov them," says he, "just repate one ov them, and I'll show you how to catapomphericate it in two shakes."

"Why then," says the Pope, "myself disremimbers the particlar passidges they allidge out ov them ould felleys," says he, "though sure enough they're more numerous nor edifying,—so we'll jist suppose that a heretic was to find sich a saying as this in Austin, 'Every sensible man knows that thransubstantiation is a lie,'—or this out of Tertullian or Plutarch, 'the bishop ov Rome is a common imposther,'—now tell me, could you answer him?"

"As easy as kiss," says his Riv'rence. "In the first, we're to understand that the exprission, 'Every sinsible man,' signifies simply, 'every man that judges by his nath'ral sinses'; and we all know that nobody follying them seven deludhers could ever find out the mysthery that's in it, if somebody did n't come in to his assistance wid an eighth sinse, which is the only sinse to be depended on, being the sinse ov the Church. So that, regarding the first quotation which your Holiness has supposed, it makes clane for us, and tee-totally agin the heretics."

"That's the explanation sure enough," says his Holiness; "and now what div you say to my being a common imposther?"

"Faix, I think," says his Riv'rence, "wid all submission to the better judgment ov the learned father that your Holiness has quoted, he'd have been a thrifle nearer the thruth, if he had said that the bishop ov

Rome is the grand imposther and top-sawyer in that line over us all."

"What do you mane?" says the Pope, getting quite red in the face.

"What would I mane," says his Riv'rence, as composed as a docther ov physic, "but that your Holiness is at the head ov all them, — troth I had a'most forgot I wasn't a bishop myself," says he, the deludher was going to say, as the head of all *uz*, "that has the gift ov laving on hands. For sure," says he, "imposther and *imposithir* is all one, so you're only to undherstand *manuum*, and the job is done. Auvuich!" says he, "if any heretic 'ud go for to cast up sich a passidge as that agin me, I'd soon give him a p'lite art ov cutting a stick to welt his own back wid."

"'Pon my apostolical word," says the Pope, "you've cleared up them two pints in a most satiswhactery manner."

"You see," says his Riv'rence, — by this time they wor mixing their third tumbler, — "the writings of them Fathers is to be thrated wid great veneration; and it 'ud be the height ov presumption in any one to sit down to interpret them widout providing himself wid a genteel assortment ov the best figures of rhetoric, sich as mettonymy, hyperbol, cattychraysis, prolipsis, mettylipsis, superbaton, pollysyndreton, husthcronprotheron, prosodypeia and the like, in ordher that he may never be at a loss for shuitable sintiments when he comes to their high-flown passidges. For unless we thrate them Fathers liberally to a handsome allowance ov thropes and figures they 'd set up heresy at onc't, so they would."

"It's thru for you," says the Pope; "the figures ov spache is the pillars ov the Church."

"Bedad," says his Riv'rence, "I dunna what we'd do widout them at all."

"Which one do you prefir?" says the Pope; "that is," says he, "which figure of spache do you find most usefullest when you're hard set?"

"Metaphour's very good," says his Riv'rence, "and so's mettonymy, — and I've known prosodypeia stand to me at a pinch mighty well, — but for a constancy, superbaton's the figure for my money. Devil be in me," says he, "but I'd prove black white as fast as a horse 'ud throt wid only a good stick ov superbaton."

"Faix," says the Pope, wid a sly look, "you'd need to have it backed, I judge, wid a small piece of assurance."

"Well now, jist for that word," says his Riv'rence, "I'll prove it widout aither one or other. Black," says he, "is one thing and white is another thing. You don't conthravene that? But everything is aither one thing or another thing; I defy the Apostle Paul to get over that dilemma. Well! If anything be one thing, well and good; but if it be another thing, then it's plain it isn't both things, and so can't be two things, — nobody can deny that. But what can't be two things must be one thing, — *Ergo*, whether it's one thing or another thing it's all one. But black is one thing and white is another thing, — *Ergo*, black and white is all one. *Quod erat demonsthrandum.*"

"Stop a bit," says the Pope, "I can't althegither give in to your second miner — no — your second major."

says he, and he stopped. "Faix, then," says he, getting confused, "I don't rightly remimber where it was exactly that I thought I seen the flaw in your premises. Howsomdiver," says he, "I don't deny that it's a good conclusion, and one that 'ud be ov materil service to the Church if it was dhrawn wid a little more distinctiveness."

"I'll make it as plain as the nose on your Holiness's face, by superbaton," says his Riv'rence. "My adversary says, black is not another color, that is white? Now that's jist a parallel passidge wid the one out ov Tartulion that me and Hayes smashed the heretics on in Clarendon Sthreet. 'This is my body, that is, the figure ov my body.' That's a superbaton, and we showed that it ought n't to be read that way at all but this way, 'This figure of my body *is* my body.' Jist so wid my adversary's proposition, it must n't be undherstood the way it reads, by no manner of manes; but it's to be taken this way, — 'Black, that is, white, is not another color,' — green, if you like, or orange, by dad, for anything I care, for my case is proved. 'Black,' that is, 'white,' lave out the 'that,' by sinnalayphy, and you have the orthodox conclusion, 'Black is white,' or by convarsion, 'White is black.'"

"It's as clear as mud," says the Pope.

"Bedad," says his Riv'rence, "I'm in great humor for disputin' to-night. I wisht your Holiness was a heretic jist for two minutes," says he, "till you'd see the flaking I'd give you!"

"Well, then, for the fun o' the thing suppose me my namesake, if you like," says the Pope, laughing, "though, by Jayminy," says he, "he's not one that I take much pride out ov."

"Very good, — devil a bitther joke ever I had," says his Riv'rence. "Come, then, Misther Pope," says he, "hould up that purty face ov yours, and answer me this question. Which 'ud be the biggest lie, if I said I seen a turkey-cock lying on the broad ov his back, and picking the stars out ov the sky, or if I was to say that I seen a gandher in the same intherrestin' posture, ray-creating himself wid similar asthronomical experiments? Answer me that, you ould swaddler?" says he.

"How durst you call me a swaddler, sir?" says the Pope, forgetting, the dear man, the part that he was acting.

"Don't think to bully me!" says his Riv'rence. "I always daar to spake the truth, and it's well known that you're nothing but a swaddling ould sent ov a saint," says he, never letting on to persave that his Holiness had forgot what they were agreed on.

"By all that's good," says the Pope, "I often hard ov the imperance ov you Irish afore," says he, "but I never expected to be called a saint in my own house, either by Irishman or Hottentot. I'll till you what, Misther Maguire," says he, "if you can't keep a civil tongue in your head, you had betther be walking off wid yourself; for I beg lave to give you to undherstand, that it won't be for the good ov your health if you call me by sich an outprobrious epithet again," says he.

"O, indeed! then things is come to a purty pass," says his Riv'rence, (the dear funny soul that he ever was!) "when the lik ov you compares one of the

Maguires ov Tempo wid a wild Ingine! Why, man alive, the Maguires was kings ov Fermanagh three thousand years afore your grandfather, that was the first ov your breed that ever wore shoes and stockings" (I 'm bound to say, in justice to the poor Prodesan, that this was all spoken by his Riv'rence by way of a figure ov spache), "was sint his Majesty's arrand to cultivate the friendship of Prince Lee Boo in Botteney Bay! O, Bryan dear," says he, letting on to cry, "if you were alive to hear a *boddagh Sassenagh* like this casting up his counthry to me ov the name ov Maguire."

"In the name ov God," says the Pope, very solemniously, "what *is* the maning ov all this at all at all?" says he.

"Sure," says his Riv'rence, whispering to him across the table, — "sure, you know we 're acting a conthrawarsy, and you tuck the part ov the Prodesan champion. You would n't be angry wid me, I 'm sure, for sarving out the heretic to the best ov my ability."

"O begad, I had forgot," says the Pope, the goodnatured ould crethur; "sure enough, you were only taking your part as a good Milesian Catholic ought agin the heretic Sassenagh. Well," says he, "fire away now, and I 'll put up wid as many conthroversial compliments as you plase to pay me."

"Well, then, answer me my question, you santimonious ould dandy," says his Riv'rence.

"In troth, then," says the Pope, "I dunna which 'ud be the biggest lie, to my mind," says he; "the one appears to be about as big a bounce as the other."

"Why, then, you poor simpleton," says his Riv'rence, "don't you persave that forbye the advantage the gandher 'ud have in the length ov his neck, it 'ud be next to empossible for the turkey-cock lying thataway to see what he was about, by rason ov his djollars and other accouthrements hanging back over his eyes? The one about as big a bounce as the other! O you misfortunate crethur! if you had ever larned your A B C iu theology, you'd have known that there's a differ betuxt them two lies so great, that, begad, I would n't wondher if it 'ud make a balance ov five years in purgathory to the sowl that 'ud be in it. Ay, and if it was n't that the Church is too liberal entirely, so she is, it 'ud cost his heirs and succissors betther nor ten pounds to have him out as soon as the other. Get along, man, and take half a year at dogmatical theology: go and read your Dens, you poor dunce, you!"

"Raaly," says the Pope, "you're making the heretic shoes too hot to hould me. I wundher how the Prodesans can stand afore you at all."

"Don't think to delude me," says his Riv'rence, "don't think to back out ov your challenge now," says he, "but come to the scratch like a man, if you are a man, and answer me my question. What's the rason, now, that Julius Cæsar and the Vargin Mary was born upon the one day,—answer me that, if you would n't be hissed off the platform?"

Well, my dear, the Pope could n't answer it, and he had to acknowledge himself sacked. Then he axed his Riv'rence to tell him the rason himself; and Father Tom communicated it to him in Latin. But as that is a very deep question, I never hard what the answer was, except that I'm tould it was so mysterious, it made the Pope's hair stand on end. But there's two o'clock, and I'll be late for the lecthir.

III.

HOW FATHER TOM MADE A HARE OF HIS HOLINESS IN LATIN.

O Docther Whateley, Docther Whateley, I'm sure I'll never die another death, if I don't die aither ov consumption or production! I ever and always thought that asthronomy was the hardest science that was till now, — and, it's no lie I'm telling you, the same asthronomy is a tough enough morsel to brake a man's fast upon, — and geolidgy is middling and hard too, — and hydherastatics is no joke, — but ov all the books ov science that ever was opened and shut, that book upon P'litical Econimy lifts the pins! Well, well, if they wait till they persuade me that taking a man's rints out ov the counthry, and spinding them in forrain parts is n't doing us out ov the same, they'll wait a long time in truth. But you're waiting, I see, to hear how his Riv'rence and his Holiness got on after finishing the disputation I was telling you of. Well, you see, my dear, when the Pope found he could n't hould a candle to Father Tom in theology and logic, he thought he'd take the shine out ov him in Latin anyhow: so says he, "Misther Maguire," says he, "I quite agree wid you that it's not lucky for us to be spaking on them deep subjects in sich langidges as the evil spirits is acquainted wid; and," says he, "I think it 'ud be no harm for us to spake from this out in Latin," says he, "for fraid the devil 'ud undherstand what we are saying."

"Not a hair I care," says Father Tom, "whether they undherstand what we're saying or not, as long as we keep off that last pint we wer discussing, and one or two others. Listners never hear good ov themselves," says he, "and if Belzhebub takes anything amiss that aither you or me says in regard ov himself or his faction, let him stand forrid like a man, and never fear, I'll give him his answer. Howandiver, if it's for a taste ov classic conwersation you are, jist to put us in mind ov ould Cordarius," says he, "here's at you." And wid that he lets fly at his Holiness wid his health in Latin.

"Vesthræ Sanctitatis salutem volo," says he.

"Vesthræ Revirintiæ salutritati bibo," says the Pope to him again (haith, it's no joke, I tell you, to remimber sich a power ov larning). "Here's to you wid the same," says the Pope, in the raal Ciceronian. "Nunc poculum alterhum imple," says he.

"Cum omni jucunditate in vita," says his Riv'rence. "Cum summá concupiscintiá et animositate," says he, as much as to say, "Wid all the veins ov my heart, I'll do that same,"—and so wid that they mix'd their fourth gun apiece.

"Aqua vitæ vesthra sane est liquor admirabilis," says the Pope.

"Verum est pro te,—it's thrue for you,"—says his Riv'rence, forgetting the idyim ov the Latin phwraseology in a manner.

"Prava est tua Latinitas, domine," says the Pope, finding fault like wid his etymology.

"Parva culpa mihi," "small blame to me, that 's," says his Riv'rence, "nam multum laboro in partibus interioribus," says he — the dear man! that never was at a loss for an excuse!

"Quid tibi incommodi?" says the Pope, axing him what ailed him.

"Habesne id quod Anglicè vocamus a looking-glass," says his Riv'rence.

"Immo, habeo speculum splendidissimum subther operculum pyxidis hujus starnutatoriæ," says the Pope, pulling out a beautiful goold snuff-box, wid a looking-glass in undher the lid — "Subther operculum pyxidis hujus starnutatorii — no — starnutatoriæ — quam dono accepi ab Arch-duce Austhriaco siptuagisima prœtheritâ," says he, — as much as to say that he got the box in a prisint from the Queen ov Spain last Lint, if I rightly remimber.

Well, Father Tom laughed like to burst. At last, says he, "Pather Sancte," says he, "sub errore jaces. 'Looking-glass' apud nos habet significationem quamdam peculiarem ex tempore dici dependentem," — there was a sthring ov accusatives for yes! — "nam mane speculum sonat," says he, "post prandium vero mat — mat — mat" — sorra be in me but I disremimber the classic appellivation ov the same article. Howandiver, his Riv'rence went on explaining himself in such a way as no scholar could mistake. "Vesica mea," says he, "ab illo ultimo eversore distenditur, donec similis est rumpere. Verbis apertis," says he, "Vesthræ

Sanctitatis præsentia salvata, aquam facere valde desidhero."

"Ho, ho, ho!" says the Pope, grabbing up his box, "si inquinavisses meam pyxidem, excimnicari debuisses — Hillo, Anthony," says he to his head butler, "fetch Misther Maguire a —"

"You spoke first!" says his Riv'rence, jumping off his sate, — "you spoke first in the vernacular! I take Misther Anthony to witness," says he.

"What else would you have me to do?" says the Pope, quite dogged like to see himself bate thataway at his own waypons. "Sure," says he, "Anthony would n't undherstand a B from a bull's foot, if I spoke to him any other way."

"Well, then," says his Riv'rence, "in considheration ov the needcessity," says he, "I 'll let you off for this time! but mind now, afther I say *præstho*, the first ov us that spakes a word ov English is the hare — *præstho!*"

Neither ov them spoke for near a minit, considering wid themselves how they were to begin sich a great thrial ov shkill. At last, says the Pope, — the blessed man, only think how 'cute it was ov him! — "Domine Maguire," says he, "valce desidhero, certiorem fieri de significatione istius verbi *eversor* quo jam jam usus es" — (well, surely I *am* the boy for the Latin!)

"*Eversor*, id est cyathus," says his Riv'rence, "nam apud nos *tumbleri* seu eversores, dicti sunt ab evertendo ceremoniam inter amicos; non, ut Temperantiæ Societatis frigidis fautoribus placet, ab evertendis ipsis potatoribus." (It 's not every masther undher the Buord,

I tell you, could carry sich a car-load ov the dead languidges.) "In agro vero Louthiano et Midensi," says he, "nomine gaudent quodam secundum linguam Anglicanam significante bombardam seu tormentum; quia ex eis tanquam ex telis jaculatoriis liquorem facibus immittere solent. Etiam inter hæreticos illos melanostomos" (that was a touch ov Greek). "Presbyterianos Septentrionales, qui sunt terribiles potatores, Cyathi dicti sunt *faceres*, et dimidium Cyathi *hæf-a-glessus*. Dimidium Cyathi verò apud Metropolitanos Hibernicos dicitur *dandy*."

"En verbum Anglicanum!" says the Pope, clapping his hands, — "leporem te fecisti"; as much as to say that he had made a hare of himself.

"*Dandæus, dandæus* verbum erat," says his Riv'rence, — O, the dear man, but it's himself that was handy ever and always at getting out ov a hobble, — "*dandæus* verbum erat," says he, "quod dicturus eram, cum me intherpillavisti."

"Ast ego dico," says the Pope very sharp, "quod verbum erat *dandy*."

"Per tibicinem qui coram Mose modulatus est," says his Riv'rence, "id flagellat mundum! *Dandæus* dixi, et tu dicis *dandy*; ergo tu es lepus, non ego — Ah, ha! Saccavi vesthram Sanctitatem!"

"Mendacium est!" says the Pope, quite forgetting himself, he was so mad at being sacked before the sarvints.

Well, if it hadn't been that his Holiness was in it, Father Tom 'ud have given him the contints of his tumbler betuxt the two eyes, for calling him a liar; and, in troth, it's very well it was in Latin the offince was conweyed, for, if it had been in the vernacular, there's no saying what 'ud ha' been the consequence. His Riv'rence was mighty angry anyhow. "Tu senex lathro," says he, "quomodo audes me mendacem prædicare?"

"Et, tu, sacrilege nebulo," says the Pope, "quomodo audacitatem habeas, me Dei in terris vicarium, lathronem conwiciari?"

"Interroga circumcirca," says his Riv'rence.

"Abi ex ædibus meis," says the Pope.

"Abi tu in malam crucem," says his Riv'rence.

"Excimnicabo te," says the Pope.

"Diabolus curat," says his Riv'rence.

"Anathema sis," says the Pope.

"Oscula meum pod —" says his Riv'rence — but, my dear, afore he could finish what he was going to say, the Pope broke out into the vernacular, "Get out o' my house, you reprobate!" says he, in sich a rage that he could contain himself widin the Latin no longer.

"Ha, ha, ha! — ho, ho, ho!" says his Riv'rence. "Who's the hare now, your Holiness? O, by this and by that, I've sacked you clane! Clane and clever I've done it, and no mistake! You see what a bit of desate will do wid the wisest, your Holiness, — sure it was joking I was, on purpose to aggravate you, — all's fair, you know, in love, law, and conthravarsy. In troth if I'd thought you'd have taken it so much to heart, I'd have put my head into the fire afore I'd have said a word to offend you," says he, for he seen that the Pope was very vexed. "Sure, God forbid, that I'd say anything agin your Holiness, barring it was in fun : for are n't you the father ov the faithful, and the thrue vicar ov God upon earth? And are n't I ready to go down on my two knees this blessed minit and beg your apostolical pardon for every word that I said to your displasement?"

"Are you in arnest that it is in fun you wer?" says the Pope.

"May I never die if I are n't," says his Riv'rence. "It was all to provoke your Holiness to commit a brache ov the Latin, that I tuck the small liberties I did," says he.

"I'd have you to take care," says the Pope, "how you take sich small liberties again, or maybe you'll provoke me to commit a brache ov the pace."

"Well, and if I did," says his Riv'rence, "I know a sartan preparation ov chymicals that's very good for curing a brache either in Latinity or friendship."

"What's that?" says the Pope, quite mollified, and sitting down again at the table that he had ris from in the first pluff of his indignation. "What's that?" says he, "for 'pon my Epistolical 'davy, I think it 'ud n't be asy to bate this miraculous mixthir that we've been thrying to anilize this two hours back," says he, taking a mighty scientifical swig out ov the bottom ov his tumbler.

"It's good for a beginning," says his Riv'rence; "it lays a very nate foundation for more sarious operation: but we're now arrived at a pariod ov the evening when it's time to procced wid our shuperstructure by compass and square, like free and excipted masons as we both are."

My time's up for the present; but I'll tell you the rest in the evening at home.

IV.

HOW FATHER TOM AND HIS HOLINESS DISPUTED AT METAPHYSICS AND ALGEBRA.

God be wid the time when I went to the classical seminary ov Firdramore! when I'd bring my sod o' turf undher my arm, and sit down on my shnug boss o' straw, wid my back to the masther and my shins to the fire, and score my sum in Dives's denominations ov the double rule o' three, or play fox and geese wid purty Jane Cruise that sat next me, as plisantly as the day was long, widout any one so much as saying, "Mikey Hefferman, what's that you're about?"—for ever since I was in the one lodge wid poor ould Mat I had my own way in his school as free as ever I had in my mother's shebeen.

God be wid them days, I say again, for it's althered times wid me, I judge, since I got undher Carlisle and Whateley. Sich sthrictness! sich ordher! sich dhrilling, and lecthiring, and tuthoring as they do get on wid! I wisht to gracious the one half ov their rules and regilations was sunk in the say. And they're getting so sthrict too about having fair play for the heretic childer! We've to have no more schools in the chapels, nor masses in the schools. O, by this and by that, it'll never do at all!

The ould plan was twenty times betther: and, for my own part, if it was n't that the clargy supports them in a manner, and the grant's a thing not easily done widout these hard times, I'd see if I could n't get a sheltered spot nigh hand the chapel, and set up again on the good ould principle: and faix, I think our metropolitan 'ud stand to me, for I know that his Grace's motto was ever and always, that, "Ignorance is the thrue mother ov piety."

But I'm running away from my narrative entirely, so I am. "You'll plase to ordher up the housekeeper, then," says Father Tom to the Pope, "wid a pint ov sweet milk in a skillet, and the bulk ov her fist ov butther, along wid a dust ov soft sugar in a saucer, and I'll show you the way of producing a decoction that, I'll be bound, will hunt the thirst out ov every nook and corner in your Holiness's blessed carcidge."

The Pope ordhered up the ingredients, and they were brought in by the head butler.

"That'll not do at all," says his Riv'rence, "the ingredients won't combine in due proportion unless ye do as I bid yes. Send up the housekeeper," says he, "for a faymale hand is ondispinsably necessary to produce the adaption of the particles and the concurrence of the corpus'cles, widout which you might boil till morning and never fetch the cruds off ov it."

Well, the Pope whispered to his head butler, and by and by up there comes an ould faggot ov a *Cuillean*, that was enough to frighten a horse from his oats.

"Don't thry for to desave me," says his Riv'rence, "for it's no use, I tell yes. Send up the housekeeper, I bid yes: I seen her presarving gooseberries in the panthry as I came up: she has eyes as black as a sloe," says he, "and cheeks like the rose in June; and sorra taste ov this celestial mixthir shall crass the lips ov man or morteal this blessed night till she stirs the same up wid her own delicate little finger."

"Misther Maguire," says the Pope, "it's very unproper ov you to spake that way ov my housekeeper: I won't allow it, sir."

"Honor bright, your Holiness," says his Riv'rence, laying his hand on his heart.

"O, by this and by that, Misther Maguire," says the Pope, "I'll have none of your insinivations; I don't care who sees my whole household," says he; "I don't care if all the faymales undher my roof was paraded down the High Street of Room," says he.

"O, it's plain to be seen how little you care who sees them," says his Riv'rence. "You're afeard, now, if I was to see your housekeeper, that I'd say she was too handsome."

"No, I'm not!" says the Pope, "I don't care who sees her," says he. "Anthony," says he to the head butler, "bid Eliza throw her apron over her head, and come up here." Wasn't that stout in the blessed man? Well, my dear, up she came, stepping like a three-year-old, and blushing like the brake o' day: for though her apron was thrown over her head as she came forrid, till you could barely see the tip ov her chin,— more be token there was a lovely dimple in it, as I've been tould, — yet she let it shlip abit to one side, by chance like, jist as she got fornenst the fire, and if she wouldn't have given his Riv'rence a shot if he hadn't been a priest, it's no matther.

"Now, my dear," says he, "you must take that skillet, and hould it over the fire till the milk comes to a blood hate; and the way you'll know that will be by stirring it one't or twice wid the little finger ov your right hand, afore you put in the butther: not that I misdoubt," says he, "but that the same finger's fairer nor the whitest milk that ever came from the tit."

"None of your deludhering talk to the young woman, sir," says the Pope, mighty stern. "Stir the posset as he bids you, Eliza, and then be off wid yourself," says he.

"I beg your Holiness's pardon ten thousand times," says his Riv'rence, "I'm sure I meant nothing onproper; I hope I'm uncapable ov any sich dirilection of my duty," says he. "But, marciful Saver!" he cried out, jumping up on a suddent, "look behind you, your Holiness, — I'm blest but the room's on fire!"

Sure enough the candle fell down that minit, and was near setting fire to the windy-curtains, and there was some bustle, as you may suppose, getting things put to rights. And now I have to tell you ov a really onpleasant occurrence. If I was a Prodesan that was in it, I'd say that while the Pope's back was turned, Father Tom made free wid the two lips of Miss Eliza; but, upon my conscience, I believe it was a mere mistake that his Holiness fell into on account of his being an ould man and not having aither his eyesight or his hearing very parfect. At any rate, it can't be denied but that he had a sthrong imprission that sich was the case; for he wheeled about as quick as thought, jist as his Riv'rence was sitting down, and charged him wid the offince plain and plump. "Is it kissing my housekeeper before my face you are, you villain!" says he. "Go down out o' this," says he, to Miss Eliza, "and do you be packing off wid you," he says to Father Tom, "for it's not safe, so it isn't, to have the likes ov you in a house where there's temptation in your way."

"Is it me?" says his Riv'rence; "why what would your Holiness be at, at all? Sure I wasn't doing no such thing."

"Would you have me doubt the evidence ov my sinses?" says the Pope; "would you have me doubt the testimony of my eyes and ears?" says he.

"Indeed I would so," says his Riv'rence, "if they pretend to have informed your Holiness ov any sich foolishness."

"Why," says the Pope, "I've seen you afther kissing Eliza as plain as I see the nose on your face; I heard the smack you gave her as plain as ever I heard thundher."

"And how do you know whether you see the nose on my face or not?" says his Riv'rence, "and how do you know whether what you thought was thundher, was thundher at all? Them operations on the sinses," says he, "comprises only particular corporal emotions, connected wid sartain confused perciptions called sinsations, and is n't to be depended upon at all. If we were to follow them blind guides we might jist as well turn heretics at onc't. 'Pon my secret word, your Holiness, it's neither charitable nor orthodox ov you to set up the testimony ov your eyes and ears agin the characther ov a clergyman. And now, see how aisy it is to explain all them phwenomena that perplexed you. I ris and went over beside the young woman because the skillet was boiling over, to help her to save the dhrop ov liquor that was in it; and as for the noise you heard, my dear man, it was neither more nor less nor myself dhrawing the cork out ov this blissid bottle."

"Don't offer to thrape that upon me!" says the Pope; "here's the cork in the bottle still, as tight as a wedge."

"I beg your pardon," says his Riv'rence, "that's not the cork at all," says he; "I dhrew the cork a good two minits ago, and it's very purtily spitted on the end ov this blessed corkshcrew at this prisint moment; howandiver you can't see it, because it's only its real prisince that's in it. But that appearance that you call a cork," says he, "is nothing but the outward spacies and external qualities of the cortical nathur. Them's nothing but the accidents of the cork that you're looking at and handling; but, as I tould you afore, the real cork's dhrew and is here prisint on the end ov this nate little insthrument, and it was the noise I made in dhrawing it, and nothing else, that you mistook for the sound ov the *pogue*."

You know there was no conthravening what he said; and the Pope couldn't openly deny it. Howandiver he thried to pick a hole in it this way. "Granting," says he, "that there is the differ you say betwixt the reality ov the cork and these cortical accidents; and that it's quite possible, as you allidge, that the thrue cork is really prisint on the end ov the shcrew, while the accidents keep the mouth ov the bottle stopped — still," says he, "I can't undherstand, though willing to acquit you, how the dhrawing ov the real cork, that's onpalpable and widout accidents, could produce the accident of that sinsible explosion I heard jist now."

"All I can say," says his Riv'rence, "is that it was a rale accident, anyhow."

"Ay," says the Pope, "the kiss you gev Eliza, you mane."

"No," says his Riv'rence, "but the report I made."

"I don't doubt you," says the Pope.

"No cork could be dhrew with less noise," says his Riv'rence.

"It would be hard for anything to be less nor nothing, barring algebra," says the Pope.

"I can prove to the conthrary," says his Riv'rence. "This glass ov whiskey is less nor that tumbler ov punch, and that tumbler ov punch is nothing to this jug ov *scaltheen*."

"Do you judge by superficial misure or by the liquid contents?" says the Pope.

"Don't stop me, betwixt my premises and my conclusion," says his Riv'rence: "*Ergo*, this glass ov whiskey is less nor nothing; and for that raison I see no harm in life in adding it to the contents ov the same jug, just by way ov a frost-nail."

"Adding what's less nor nothing," says the Pope, "is subtraction according to algebra, so here goes to make the rule good," says he, filling his tumbler wid the blessed stuff, and sitting down again at the table, for the anger did n't stay two minits on him, the good-hearted ould sowl.

"Two minuses make one plus," says his Riv'rence, as ready as you plase, "and that 'll account for the increased dayerement I mane to take the liberty of producing in the same mixed quantity," says he, follying his Holiness's epistolical example.

"By all that's good," says the Pope, "that's the best stuff I ever tasted; you call it a mix'd quantity, but I say it's prime."

"Since it's ov the first ordher, then," says his Riv'rence, "we'll have the less deffeequilty in reducing it to a simple equation."

"You'll have no fractions at my side anyhow," says the Pope. "Faix, I'm afeared," says he, "it's only too aisy ov solution our sum is like to be."

"Never fear for that," says his Riv'rence, "I've a good stick ov surds here in the bottle; for I tell you it will take us a long time to exthract the root ov it, at the rate we're going on."

"What makes you call the blessed quart an irrational quantity?" says the Pope.

"Because it's too much for one and too little for two," says his Riv'rence.

"Clear it ov its coefficient, and we'll thry," says the Pope.

"Hand me over the exponent then," says his Riv'rence.

"What's that?" says the Pope.

"The sherew, to be sure," says his Riv'rence.

"What for?" says the Pope.

"To dhraw the cork," says his Riv'rence.

"Sure, the cork's dhrew," says the Pope.

"But the sperets can't get out on account ov the accidents that's stuck in the neck ov the bottle," says his Riv'rence.

"Accident ought to be passable to sperit," says the Pope, "and that makes me suspect that the reality ov the cork's in it afther all."

"That's a barony-masia," says his Riv'rence, "and I'm not bound to answer it. But the fact is, that it's the accidents ov the sperits too that's in it, and the reality's passed out through the cortical spacies, as you say; for, you may have observed, we've both been in real good sperits ever since the cork was dhrawn, and where else would the real sperits come from if they wouldn't come out ov the bottle?"

"Well, then," says the Pope, "since we've got the reality, there's no use throubling ourselves wid the accidents."

"O, begad," says his Riv'rence, "the accidents is very essential too; for a man may be in the best ov good sperits, as far as his immaterial part goes, and yet need the accidental qualities ov good liquor to hunt the sinsible thirst out ov him." So he dhraws the cork in earnest, and sets about brewing the other skillet ov *scaltheen*; but, faiz, he had to get up the ingradients this time by the hands ov ould Moley; though devil a taste ov her little finger he'd let widin a yard ov the same coction.

But, my dear, here's the "Freeman's Journal," and we'll see what's the news afore we finish the residuary proceedings of their two Holinesses.

V.

THE REASON WHY FATHER TOM WAS NOT MADE A CARDINAL.

Hurroo, my darlings! — did n't I tell you it 'ud never do? Success to bould John Tuam and the ould siminary ov Firdramore! O, more power to your Grace every day you rise, 't is you that has broken their Boord into shivers undher your feet! Sure, and is n't it a proud day for Ireland, this blessed feast ov the chair ov Saint Pether? Is n't Carlisle and Whateley smashed to pieces, and their whole college of swaddling teachers knocked into smidhereens. John Tuam, your sowl, has tuck his pasthoral staff in his hand and beathen them out o' Connaught as fast as ever Pathric druve the sarpints into Clew Bay.

Poor ould Mat Kevanagh, if he was alive this day, 't is he would be the happy man. "My curse upon their g'ographies and Bibles," he used to say; "where's the use ov perplexing the poor childre wid what we don't undherstand ourselves?" No use at all, in troth, and so I said from the first myself.

Well, thank God and his Grace, we 'll have no more thrigonomethry nor scripther in Connaught. We 'll hould our lodges every Saturday night, as we used to do, wid our chairman behind the masther's desk, and we 'll hear our mass every Sunday morning wid the blessed priest standing afore the same.

I wisht to goodness I had n't parted wid my Seven Champions ov Christendom and Freney the Robber:

they're books that'll be in great requist in Leithrim as soon as the pasthoral gets wind. Glory be to God! I've done wid their leethirs, — they may all go and be d—d wid their consumption and production.

I'm off to Tallymactaggart before daylight in the morning, where I'll thry whether a sod or two o' turf can't consume a cart-load ov heresy, and whether a weekly meeting ov the lodge can't produce a new thayory ov rints.

But afore I take my lave ov you, I may as well finish my story about poor Father Tom that I hear is coming up to slate the heretics in Adam and Eve during the Lint.

The Pope — and indeed it ill became a good Catholic to say anything agin him — no more would I, only that his Riv'rence was in it — but you see the fact ov it is, that the Pope was as envious as ever he could be, at seeing himself sacked right and left by Father Tom; and bate out o' the face, the way he was, on every science and subjec' that was started. So, not to be outdone altogether, he says to his Riv'rence, "you're a man that's fond of the brute crayation, I hear, Misther Maguire?"

"I don't deny it," says his Riv'rence. "I've dogs that I'm willing to run agin any man's, ay, or to match them agin any other dogs in the world for genteel edication and polite manners," says he.

"I'll hould you a pound," says the Pope, "that I've a quadhruped in my possession that's a wiser baste nor any dog in your kennel."

"Done," says his Riv'rence, and they staked the money.

"What can this larned quadhruped o' yours do?" says his Riv'rence.

"It's my mule," says the Pope, "and, if you were to offer her goolden oats and clover off the meadows o' Paradise, sorra taste ov aither she'd let pass her teeth till the first mass is over every Sunday or holiday in the year."

"Well, and what 'ud you say if I showed you a baste ov mine," says his Riv'rence, "that, instead ov fasting till first mass is over only, fasts out the whole four-and-twenty hours ov every Wednesday and Friday in the week as reg'lar as a Christian?"

"O, be asy, Masther Maguire," says the Pope.

"You don't b'lieve me, don't you?" says his Riv'-rence; "very well, I'll soon show you whether or no." And he put his knuckles in his mouth, and gev a whistle that made the Pope stop his fingers in his ears. The aycho, my dear, was hardly done playing wid the cobwebs in the cornish, when the door flies open, and in jumps Spring. The Pope happened to be sitting next the door, betuxt him and his Riv'rence, and, may I never die, if he did n't clear him, thriple crown and all, at one spring. "God's presence be about us!" says the Pope, thinking it was an evil spirit come to fly away wid him for the lie that he had told in regard ov his mule (for it was nothing more nor a thrick that consisted in grazing the brute's teeth): but, seeing it was only one ov the greatest beauties ov a greyhound that he'd ever laid his epistolical eyes on, he soon recovered ov his fright, and began to pat him, while Father Tom ris and went to the sideboord, where he cut a slice ov pork, a slice ov beef, a slice ov mutton, and a slice ov salmon, and put them all on a plate thegither. "Here, Spring, my man," says he, setting the plate down afore him on the hearthstone, "here's your supper for you this blessed Friday night." Not a word more he said nor what I tell you; and, you may believe it or not, but it's the blessed truth that the dog, afther jist tasting the salmon, and spitting it out again, lifted his nose out o' the plate, and stood wid his jaws wathering, and his tail wagging, looking up in his Riv'rence's face, as much as to say, "Give me your absolution, till I hide them temptations out o' my sight."

"There's a dog that knows his duty," says his Riv'rence; "there's a baste that knows how to conduct himself aither in the parlor or the field. You think him a good dog, looking at him here: but I wisht you seen him on the side ov Sleeve-an-Eirin! Be my soul, you'd say the hill was running away from undher him. O, I wisht you had been wid me," says he, never letting on to see the dog stale, "one day, last Lent, that I was coming from mass. Spring was near a quarther ov a mile behind me, for the childher was delaying him wid bread and butther at the chapel door; when a lump ov a hare jumped out ov the plantations ov Grouse Lodge and ran acrass the road; so I gev the whilloo, and knowing that she'd take the rise of the hill, I made over the ditch, and up through Mullaghcashel as hard as I could pelt, still keeping her in view, but afore I had gone a perch, Spring seen her, and away the two went like the wind, up Drumrewy, and down Clooneen, and over the river, widout his being able onc't to turn her. Well, I run on till I come to the Diffagher, and through it I went, for the wather was low and I did n't mind being wet shod, and out on the other side, where I got up on a ditch, and seen sich a coorse as I 'll be bound to say was never seen afore or since. If Spring turned that hare onc't that day, he turned her fifty times, up and down, back and for'ard, throughout and about. At last he run her right into the big quarryhole in Mullaghbawn, and when I went up to look for her fud, there I found him sthretched on his side, not able to stir a foot, and the hare lying about an inch afore his nose as dead as a door-nail, and divil a mark of a tooth upon her. Eh, Spring, is n't that thrue?" says he. Jist at that minit the clock sthruck twelve, and, before you could say thrap-sticks, Spring had the plateful of mate consaled. "Now," says his Riv'rence, "hand me over my pound, for I 've won my bate fairly."

"You 'll excuse me," says the Pope, pocketing his money, "for we put the clock half an hour back, out ov compliment to your Riv'rence," says he, "and it was Sathurday morning afore he came up at all."

"Well, it 's no matther," says his Riv'rence, putting back his pound-note in his pocket-book. "Only," says he, "it 's hardly fair to expect a brute baste to be so well skilled in the science ov chronology."

In troth his Riv'rence was badly used in the same bet, for he won it clever; and, indeed, I 'm afeard the shabby way he was thrated had some effect in putting it into his mind to do what he did. "Will your Holiness take a blast ov the pipe?" says he, dhrawing out his dhudeen.

"I never smoke," says the Pope, "but I have n't the least objection to the smell of the tobaccay."

"O, you had betther take a dhraw," says his Riv'rence, "it'll relish the dhrink, that 'ud be too luscious entirely, widout something to flavor it."

"I had thoughts," said the Pope, wid the laste sign ov a hiccup on him, "ov getting up a broiled bone for the same purpose."

"Well," says his Riv'rence, "a broiled bone 'ud do no manner ov harm at this present time; but a smoke," says he, "'ud flavor both the devil and the dhrink."

"What sort o' tobaccay is it that's in it?" says the Pope.

"Raal nagur-head," says his Riv'rence, "a very mild and salubrious spacies ov the philosophic weed."

"Then, I don't care if I do take a dhraw," says the Pope. Then Father Tom held the coal himself till his Holiness had the pipe lit; and they sat widout saying anything worth mentioning for about five minutes.

At last the Pope says to his Riv'rence, "I dunna what gev me this plaguy hiccup," says he. "Dhrink about," says he — "Begorra," he says, "I think I'm getting merrier 'an 's good for me. Sing us a song, your Riv'rence," says he.

Father Tom then sung him Monatagrenage and the Bunch o' Rushes, and he was mighty well pleased wid both, keeping time wid his hands, and joining in the choruses, when his hiccup 'ud let him. At last, my dear, he opens the lower button ov his waistcoat, and the top one of his waistband, and calls to Masther Anthony to lift up one ov the windys. "I dunna what's wrong wid me, at all at all," says he; "I'm mortal sick."

"I thrust," says his Riv'rence, "the pasthry that you ate at dinner has n't disagreed wid your Holiness's stomach."

"O my! oh!" says the Pope, "what's this at all?" gasping for breath, and as pale as a sheet, wid a could swate bursting out over his forehead, and the palms ov his hands spread out to cotch the air. "O my! O my!" says he, "fetch me a basin! — Don't spake to me. Oh! — oh! — blood alive! — O, my head, my head, hould my head! — oh! — ubh! — I'm poisoned! — ach!"

"It was them plaguy pasthries," says his Riv'rence. "Hould his head hard," says he, "and clap a wet cloth over his timples. If you could only thry another dhraw o' the pipe, your Holiness, it 'ud set you to rights in no time."

"Carry me to bed," says the Pope, "and never let me see that wild Irish priest again. I'm poisoned by his manes — ubplsch! — ach! — ach! — He dined wid Cardinal Wayld yestherday," says he, "and he's bribed him to take me off. Send for a confessor," says he, "for my latther end's approaching. My head's like to split — so it is! — O my! O my! — ubplsch! — ach!"

Well, his Riv'rence never thought it worth his while to make him an answer; but, when he seen how ungratefully he was used, afther all his throuble in making the evening agreeable to the ould man, he called Spring, and put the but-end ov the second bottle into his pocket, and left the house widout once wishing "Good night, an' plaisant dhrames to you"; and, in troth, not one of *them* axed him to lave them a lock ov his hair.

That's the story as I heard it tould: but myself does n't b'lieve over one half of it. Howandiver, when all 's done, it 's a shame, so it is, that he 's not a bishop this blessed day and hour: for, next to the goiant ov Saint Garlath's, he 's out and out the cleverest fellow ov the whole jing-bang.

JOHNNY DARBYSHIRE.

BY WILLIAM HOWITT.

JOHN DARBYSHIRE, or, according to the regular custom of the country, Johnny Darbyshire, was a farmer living in one of the most obscure parts of the country, on the borders of the Peak of Derbyshire. His fathers before him had occupied the same farm for generations; and as they had been Quakers from the days of George Fox, who preached there and converted them, Johnny also was a Quaker. That is, he was, as many others were, and no doubt are, habitually a Quaker. He was a Quaker in dress, in language, in attendance of their meetings, and, above all, in the unmitigated contempt which he felt and expressed for everything like fashion, for the practices of the world, for the Church, and for music and amusements. There never was a man, from the first to the present day of the society, who so thoroughly embodied and exhibited that quality attributed to the Quaker, in the rhyming nursery alphabet,—"Q was a Quaker, and would not bow down."

No, Johnny Darbyshire would not have bowed down

to any mortal power. He would have marched into the presence of the king with his hat on, and would have addressed him with just the same unembarrassed freedom as "The old chap out of the West Countrie" is made to do in the song. As to any of the more humble and conceding qualities usually attributed to the peaceful Quaker, Johnny had not an atom of those about him. Never was there a more pig-headed, arbitrary, positive, pugnacious fellow. He would argue anybody out of their opinions by the hour; he would "threep them down," as he called it, that is, point blank and with a loud voice insist on his own possession of the right, and of the sound common-sense of the matter; and if he could not convince them, would at least confound them with his obstreperous din and violence of action. That was what he called clearing the field, and not leaving his antagonist a leg to stand on. Having thus fairly overwhelmed, dumfoundered, and tired out some one with his noise, he would go off in triumph, and say to the bystanders as he went, "There, lads, you see he had n't a word to say for himself"; and truly a clever fellow must he have been who could have got a word in edgeways when Johnny had once fairly got his steam up, and was shrieking and storming like a cat-o'-mountain.

Yet had anybody told Johnny that he was no Quaker, he would have "threeped them down" that they did not know what a Quaker meant. What! were not his father, and his grandfather, and his great-grandfather before him all Quakers? Was not he born in the Society, brought up in it? Had n't he attended first-day, week-day, preparative, monthly, quarterly, and sometimes yearly meetings too, all his life? Had not he regularly and handsomely subscribed to the monthly, and the national, and the Ackworth School Stocks? Had he not been on all sorts of appointments; to visit new members, new comers into the meeting; to warn disorderly walkers; nay, had he not sate even on committees in London at yearly meetings? Had he not received and travelled with ministers when they came on religious visits into these parts? Had he not taken them in his tax-cart to the next place, and been once upset in a deep and dirty lane with a weighty ministering friend, and dislocated his collar-bone?

What? He not a Quaker! Was George Fox one, did they think; or William Penn, or Robert Barclay, indeed?

Johnny Darbyshire *was* a Quaker. He had the dress, and address, and all the outward testimonies and marks of a Quaker; nay, he was more; he was an overseer of the meeting, and broke up the meetings. Yes, and he would have them to know that he executed his office well. Ay, well indeed; without clock to look at, or without pulling out his watch, or being within hearing of any bell, or any other thing that could guide him, he would sit on the front seat of his meeting where not a word was spoken, exactly for an hour and three quarters to a minute, and then break it up by shaking hands with the Friend who sate next to him. Was not that an evidence of a religious tact and practice? And had not the Friends once when he was away, just like people in a ship which had lost both rudder and compass, gone drifting in unconsciousness from ten in the morning till three in the afternoon, and would not then have known that it was time to break up the meeting, but that somebody's servant was sent to see what had happened, and why they did not come home to dinner?

Johnny could see a sleeper as soon as any, were he ensconced in the remotest and obscurest corner of the meeting, and let him hold up his head and sleep as cleverly as he might from long habit. And did not he once give a most notable piece of advice to a *rich* Friend who was a shocking sleeper? Was not this Friend very ill, and did n't Johnny go to see him; and did n't he, when the Friend complained that he could get no sleep, and that not all the physic, the strongest opium even of the doctor's shop, could make him, — did n't Johnny Darbyshire say right slap-bang out, which not another of the plainest-spoken Friends dare have done to a rich man like that, — "Stuff and nonsense; and a fig for opium and doctor's stuff, — send, man, send for the meeting-house bench, and lie thee down on that, and I'll be bound thou 'lt sleep like one of the seven sleepers."

Undoubtedly Johnny was a Quaker; a right slap-dash Quaker of the old Foxite school; and had anybody come smiling to him in the hope of getting anything out of him, he would have said to him as George Fox said to Colonel Hackett, "Beware of hypocrisy and a rotten heart!" True, had you questioned him as to his particular religious doctrines or articles of faith, he would not have been very clear, or very ready to give you any explanation at all, for the very best of reasons, — he was not so superstitious as to have a creed. A creed! that was a rag of the old woman of Babylon. No, if you wanted to know all about doctrines and disputations, why, you might look into Barclay's Apology. There was a book big enough for you, he should think. For himself, like most of his cloth, he would confine himself to his *feelings*. He would employ a variety of choice and unique phrases; such as, "If a man want to know what religion is, he must not go running after parsons, and bishops, and all that sort of man-made ministers, blind leaders of the blind, who can talk by the hour, but about what neither man, woman, nor child, for the life of them, can tell, except when they come for their tithes, or their Easter dues, and then they speak plain enough with a vengeance. One of these Common-Prayer priests," said he, "once came to advise me about the lawfulness of paying Church-rates, and, instead of walking into my parlor, he walked through the next door, and nearly broke his neck, into the cellar. A terrible stramash of a lumber, and a plunging and a groaning we heard somewhere; and rushing out, lo and behold! it was no other than Diggory Dyson, the parish priest, who had gone headlong to the bottom of the cellar steps, and had he not cut his temples against the brass tap of a beer-barrel and bled freely, he might have died on the spot. And that was a man set up to guide the multitude! Had he been only led and guided by the Spirit of God, as a true minister should be, he would never have gone neck-foremost down my cellar steps. That's your blind leader of the blind!"

But if Johnny Darbyshire thought the "Common-Prayer priests" obscure, they must have thought him sevenfold so. Instead of doctrines and such pagan things, he talked solemnly of "centring down"; "being renewedly made sensible"; "having his mind drawn to this and that thing"; "feeling himself dipped into deep baptism"; "feeling a sense of duty"; and of "seeing, or not seeing his way clear" into this or that matter. But his master phrase was "living near to the truth"; and often, when other people thought him particularly provoking and insulting, it was only "because he hated a lie and the father of lies." Johnny thought that he lived so near to the truth, that you would have thought Truth was his next-door neighbor, or his lodger, and not living down at the bottom of her well as she long has been.

Truly was that religious world in which Johnny Darbyshire lived a most singular one. In that part of the country, George Fox had been particularly zealous and well received. A simple country people was just the people to be affected by his warm eloquence and strong manly sense. He settled many meetings there, which, however, William Penn may be said to have unsettled by his planting of Pennsylvania. These Friends flocked over thither with, or after him, and left a mere remnant behind them. This remnant — and it was like the remnant in a draper's shop, a very old-fashioned one — continued still to keep up their meetings, and carry on their affairs as steadily and gravely as Fox and his contemporaries did, if not so extensively and successfully. They had a meeting at Codnor Breach, at Monny-Ash in the Peak, at Pentridge, at Toad-hole Furnace, at Chesterfield, etc. Most of these places were thoroughly country places, some of them standing nearly alone in the distant fields; and the few members belonging to them might be seen on Sundays, mounted on strong horses, a man and his wife often on one, on saddle and pillion, or in strong tax-carts; and others, generally the young, proceeding on foot over fields and through woods, to these meetings. They were truly an old-world race, clad in very old-world garments. Arrived at their meeting, they sate generally an hour and three quarters in profound silence, for none of them had a minister in them, and then returned again. In winter they generally had a good fire in a chamber, and sate comfortably round it.

Once a month, they jogged off in similar style to one of these meetings in particular, to what they called their monthly meeting, where they paid in their subscriptions for the poor, and other needs of the society, and read over and made answers to a set of queries on the moral and religious state of their meetings. One would have thought that this business must be so very small that it would be readily despatched; but not so. Small enough, Heaven knows! it was; but then they made a religious duty of its transaction, and went through it as solemnly and deliberately as if the very salvation of the kingdom depended on it. O, what a mighty balancing of straws was there! In answering the query, whether their meetings were pretty regularly kept up and attended, though perhaps there was but half a dozen members to one meeting, yet would it be weighed and weighed again whether the phrase should be, that it was "pretty well attended," or "indifferently attended," or "attended, with some exceptions." This stupendous business having, however, at length been got through, then all the men adjourned to the room where the women had, for the time, been just as laboriously and gravely engaged; and a table was soon spread by a person agreed with, with a good substantial dinner of roast-beef and plum-pudding; and the good people grew right sociable, chatty, and even merry in their way; while, all the time in the adjoining stable, or, as in one case, in the stable under them, their steeds, often rough, wild creatures, thrust perhaps twenty into a stable without dividing stalls, were kicking, squealing, and rioting in a manner that obliged some of the good people occasionally to rise from their dinners, and endeavor to diffuse a little of their own quietness among them. Or in summer their horses would be all loose in the graveyard before the meeting, rearing, kicking, and screaming in a most furious manner; which, however, only rarely seemed to disturb the meditations of their masters and mistresses.

And to these monthly meetings over what long and dreary roads, on what dreadfully wet and wintry days, through what mud and water, did these simple and pious creatures, wrapped in great-coats and thick cloaks, and defended with oil-skin hoods, travel all their lives long? Not a soul was more punctual in attendance than Johnny Darbyshire. He was a little man, wearing a Quaker suit of drab, his coat long, his hat not cocked but slouched, and his boots well worn and well greased.

Peaceful as he sate in these meetings, yet out of them, as I have remarked, he was a very Tartar, and he often set himself to execute what he deemed justice in a very dogged and original style. We may, as a specimen, take this instance. On his way to his regular meeting he had to pass through a toll-bar; and being on Sundays exempt by law from paying at it, it may be supposed that the bar-keeper did not fling open the gate often with the best grace. One Sunday evening, however, Johnny Darbyshire had, from some cause or other, stayed late with his friends after afternoon meeting. When he passed through the toll-gate he gave his usual nod to the keeper, and was passing on; but the man called out to demand the toll, declaring that it was no longer Sunday night, but Monday morning, being past twelve o'clock.

"Nay, friend, thou art wrong," said Johnny, pulling out his watch: "see, it yet wants a quarter."

"No, I tell you," replied the keeper, gruffly, "it is past twelve. Look, there is my clock."

"Ay, friend, but thy clock, like thyself, does n't speak the truth. Like its master, it is a little too hasty. I assure thee my watch is right, for I just now compared it by the steeple-house clock in the town."

"I tell you," replied the keeper, angrily, "I 've nothing to do with your watch; I go by my clock, and there it is."

"Well, I think thou art too exact with me, my friend."

"Will you pay me or not?" roared the keeper; "you go through often enough in the devil's name without paying."

"Gently, gently, my friend," replied Johnny; "there is the money: and it 's really after twelve o'clock, thou says?"

"To be sure."

"Well, very well; then, for the next twenty-four hours I can go through again without paying?"

"To be sure; everybody knows that."

"Very well, then I now bid thee farewell." And with that, Johnny Darbyshire jogged on. The gate-keeper, chuckling at having at last extorted a double toll from the shrewd Quaker, went to bed, not on that quiet road expecting further disturbance till towards daylight; but, just as he was about to pop into bed, he heard some one ride up and cry, "Gate!"

Internally cursing the late traveller, he threw on his things and descended to open the gate, when he was astonished to see the Quaker returned.

"Thou says it really *is* past twelve, friend?"

"To be sure."

"Then open the gate: I have occasion to ride back again."

The gate flew open, Johnny Darbyshire trotted back towards the town, and the man, with double curses in his mind, returned up stairs. This time he was not so sure of exemption from interruption, for he expected the Quaker would in a while be coming back homewards again. And he was quite right. Just as he was about to put out his candle, there was a cry of "Gate." He descended, and behold the Quaker once more presented himself.

"It really *is* past twelve, thou says?"

"Umph!" grunted the fellow.

"Then, of course, I have nothing more to pay. I would not, however, advise thee to go to bed to-night, for it is so particularly fine that I propose to enjoy it by riding to and fro here a few hours."

The fellow, who now saw Johnny Darbyshire's full drift, exclaimed, "Here, for God's sake, sir, take your money back, and let me get a wink of sleep."

But Johnny refused to receive the money, observing, "If it *was* after twelve, then the money is justly thine; but I advise thee another time not to be *too* exact." And with that he rode off.

Such was his shrewd, restless, domineering character, that his old friend, the neighboring miller, a shrewd fellow too, thought there must be something in Quakerism which contributed to this, and was therefore anxious to attend their meetings, and see what it was. How great, however, was his astonishment, on accompanying Johnny, to find about half a dozen people all sitting with their hats on for a couple of hours in profound silence; except a few shufflings of feet, and blowing of noses; and then all start up, shake hands, and hurry off.

"Why, Master Darbyshire," said the dry old miller, "how is this? Do you sit without parson or clerk, and expect to learn religion by looking at your shoe-toes? By Leddy! this war n't th' way George Fox went on. He was a very talking man, or he would na ha' got such a heap of folks together, as he did. You 've clearly gotten o' th' wrong side o' th' post, Johnny, depend on 't; an' I dunna wonder now that you 've dwindled awee so."

But if Johnny was as still as a fish at the Quaker meetings, he had enough to say at home, and at the parish meetings. He had such a spice of the tyrant in him, that he could not even entertain the idea of marrying, without it must be a sort of shift for the mastery. He, therefore, not only cast his eye on one of the most high-spirited women that he knew in his own society, but actually one on the largest scale of physical dimensions. If he had one hero of his admiration more than another, it was a little dwarf at Mansfield, who used to wear a soldier's jacket, and who had taken it into his head to marry a very tall woman, whom he had reduced to such perfect subjection, that he used from time to time to evince his mastery by mounting a round table and making the wife walk round it while he belabored her lustily with a strap.

Johnny, having taken his resolve, made no circumbendibus in his addresses; but one day, as he was alone in the company of the lady, by name Lizzy Lorimer, — "Lizzy," said he, "I'll tell thee what I have been thinking about. I think thou'd make me a very good wife."

"Well," replied Lizzy; "sure, is n't that extraordinary? I was just thinking the very same thing."

"That's right! Well done, my wench, — now that's what I call hitting the nail on the head, like a right sensible woman!" cried Johnny, fetching her a slap on the shoulder, and laughing heartily. "That's doing the thing now to some tune. I'm for none of your dilly-dally ways. I once knew a young fellow that was desperately smitten by a young woman, and though he could pluck up courage enough to go and see her, he could n't summon courage enough to speak out his mind when he got there; and so he and the damsel sate opposite one another before the fire. She knew well enough all the while — you're sharp enough, you women — what he was after; and there they sate and sate, and at last he picked up a cinder off the hearth, and looking very foolish, said, 'I've a good mind to fling a cowk at thee!' At which the brave wench, in great contempt, cried, 'I'll soon fling one at thee, if thou art n't off!' That's just as thou 'd ha' done, Lizzy, and as I should n't," said Johnny, gayly, and laughing more heartily than before.

That was the sum and substance of Johnny Darbyshire's courtship. All the world said the trouble would come afterwards; but if it did come, it was not to Johnny. Never was chanticleer so crouse on his own dunghill, as Johnny Darbyshire was in his own house. He was lord and master there to a certainty. In doors and out, he shouted, hurried, ran to and fro, and made men, maids, and Lizzy herself, fly at his approach, as if he had got a whole cargo of Mercury's wings, and put them on their feet. It was the same in parish affairs; and the fame of Johnny's eloquence at vestries is loud to this day. On one occasion there was a most hot debate on the voting of a church-rate, which should embrace a new pulpit. Johnny had hurt his foot with a stub of wood as he was hurrying on his men at work in thinning a plantation. It had festered and inflamed his leg to a terrible size; but, spite of that, he ordered out his cart with a bed laid in it, and came up to the door of the vestry-room, where he caused himself to be carried in on the bed, and set on the vestry-room floor, not very distant from the clergyman. Here he waited, listening first to one speaker and then another, till the debate had grown very loud, when he gave a great hem; and all were silent, for every one knew that Johnny was going to speak.

"Now, I'll tell you what, lads," said Johnny; "you've made noise enough to frighten all the jackdaws out of the steeple, and there they are flying all about with a pretty cawarring. You've spun a yarn as long as all the posts and rails round my seven acres, and I dunna see as you've yet hedged in so much as th' owd wise men o' Gotham did, and that's a cuckoo. I've heard just one sensible word, and that was to recommend a cast-iron pulpit, in preference to a wooden 'un. As to a church-rate to repair th' owd steeple-house, why, my advice is to pull th' owd thing down, stick and stone, and mend your roads with it. It's a capital heap o' stone in it, that one must allow, — and your roads are pestilent bad. Down with the old daw-house, I say, and mend th' roads wi' 't, and set th' parson here up for a guide-post. Oh! it's a rare 'un he'd make; for he's always pointing th' way to the folks, but I never see that he moves one inch himself."

"Mr. Darbyshire," exclaimed the clergyman, in high resentment, "that is very uncivil in my presence, to say the least of it."

"Civil or uncivil," returned Johnny; "it's the truth, lad, and thou can take it just as thou likes. I did not come here to bandy compliments; so I may as well be hanged for an old sheep as for a lamb, — we'll not make two mouthfuls of a cherry; my advice is then to have a cast-iron pulpit, by all means, and while you are about it, a cast-iron parson, too. It will do just as well as our neighbor Diggory Dyson here, and a plaguy deal cheaper, for it will require neither tithes, glebe, Easter-dues, nor church-rates!"

Having delivered himself of this remarkable oration, to the great amusement of his fellow-parishioners, and the equal exasperation of the clergyman, Johnny ordered himself to be again hoisted into his cart, and rode home in great glory, boasting that he had knocked all the wind out of the parson, and if he got enough again to preach his sermon on Sunday, it would be all.

It was only on such occasions as these that Johnny Darbyshire ever appeared under the church roof. Once, on the occasion of the funeral of an old neighbor, which, for a wonder, he attended, he presented himself there, but with as little satisfaction to the clergyman, and less to himself.

He just marched into the church with his hat on, which, being removed by the clergyman's orders, Johnny declared that he had a good mind to walk out of that well of a place, and would do so only out of respect to his old neighbor. With looks of great wrath he seated himself at a good distance from the clergyman; and as this gentleman was proceeding, in none of the clearest tones, certainly, to read the appropriate service, Johnny suddenly shouted out, "Speak up, man, speak up! What art mumbling at there, man? We canna hear what thou says here!"

"Who is that?" demanded the clergyman, solemnly, and looking much as if he did not clearly perceive who it was. "Who is that who interrupts the service? I will not proceed till he be removed."

The beadle approached Johnny, and begged that he would withdraw.

"Oh!" said Johnny, aloud, so as to be heard through all the church, "I'll sit i' th' porch. I'd much rather. What's the use sitting here where one can hear nothing but a buzzing like a bee in a blossom?"

Johnny accordingly withdrew to the porch, where some of his neighbors, hurrying to him when the funeral was about to proceed from the church to the grave, said, "Mr. Darbyshire, what have you done? You'll as surely be put into th' spiritual court, as you're a living man. You'd better ax the parson's pardon, and as soon as you can."

Accordingly, as soon as the funeral was over, and the clergyman was about to withdraw, up marched Johnny to him, and said, "What, I reckon I've affronted thee with bidding thee speak up. But thou *should* speak up, man; thou should speak up, or what art perched up aloft there for. But, however, as you scollards are rayther testy, I know, in being taken up before folks, I mun beg thy pardon for 't'arno."*

"O, Mr. Darbyshire," said the clergyman, with much dignity, "that will not do, I assure you. I cannot pass over such conduct in such a manner. I shall take another course with you."

"O, just as tha' woot. I've axed thy pardon, have n't I? and if that wunna do, why, thou mun please thysen!"

Johnny actually appeared very likely to get a proper castigation this time; but, however it was, he certainly escaped. The parishioners advised the clergyman to

* For what I know.

take no notice of the offence, — everybody, they said, knew Johnny, and if he called him into the spiritual court, he would be just as bold and saucy, and might raise a good deal of public scandal. The clergyman, who, unfortunately, was but like too many country clergymen of the time, addicted to a merry glass in the village public-house, thought perhaps that this was only too likely, and so the matter dropped.

For twenty years did Johnny Darbyshire thus give free scope to tongue and hand in his parish. He ruled paramount over wife, children, house, servants, parish, and everybody. He made work go on like the flying clouds of March; and at fair and market, at meeting and vestry, he had his fling and his banter at the expense of his neighbors, as if the world was all his own, and would never come to an end. But now came an event, arising, as so often is the case, out of the merest trifle, that more than all exhibited the indomitable stiffness and obstinacy of his character.

Johnny Darbyshire had some fine, rich meadow-land, on the banks of the river Derwent, where he took in cattle and horses to graze during the summer. Hither a gentleman had sent a favorite and valuable blood mare to run a few months with her foal. He had stipulated that the greatest care should be taken of both mare and foal, and that no one, on any pretence whatever, should mount the former. All this Johnny Darbyshire had most fully promised. "Nay, he was as fond of a good bit of horse-flesh as any man alive, and he would use mare and foal just as if they were his own."

This assurance, which sounded very well indeed, was

kept by Johnny, as it proved, much more to the letter than the gentleman intended. To his great astonishment, it was not long before he one day saw Johnny Darbyshire come riding on a little shaggy horse down the village where he lived, leading the foal in a halter.

He hurried out to inquire the cause of this, too well auguring some sad mischief, when Johnny, shaking his head, said, "Ill luck, my friend, never comes alone; it's an old saying, that it never rains but it pours; and so it's been with me. T' other day I'd a son drowned, as fine a lad as ever walked in shoe-leather; and in hurrying to th' doctor, how should luck have it, but down comes th' mare with her foot in a hole, breaks her leg, and was obligated to be killed; and here's th' poor innocent foal. It's a bad job, a very bad job; but I've the worst on 't, and it canna be helped; so, prithee, say as little as thou can about it, — here's the foal, poor, dumb thing, at all events."

"But what business," cried the gentleman, enraged, and caring, in his wrath, not a button for Johnny Darbyshire's drowned son, in the exasperation of his own loss, — "but what business had you riding to the doctor, or the devil, on my mare? Did not I enjoin you, did you not solemnly promise me, that nobody should cross the mare's back?"

Johnny shook his head. He had indeed promised "to use her as his own," and he had done it to some purpose; but that was little likely to throw cold water on the gentleman's fire. It was in vain that Johnny tried the pathetic of the drowning boy; it was lost on the man who had lost his favorite mare, and who declared that he would rather have lost a thousand pounds, — a hundred was exactly her value, — and he vowed all sorts of vengeance and of law.

And he kept his word too. Johnny was deaf to paying for the mare. He had lost his boy, and his summer's run of the mare and foal, and that he thought enough for a poor man like him, as he pleased to call himself. An action was commenced against him, of which he took not the slightest notice till it came into court. These lawyers, he said, were dear chaps, he'd have nothing to do with them. But the lawyers were determined to have to do with him, for they imagined that the Quaker had a deep purse, and they longed to be poking their long, jewelled fingers to the bottom of it.

The cause actually came into court at the assizes, and the counsel for the plaintiff got up and stated the case, offering to call his evidence, but first submitted that he could not find that any one was retained on behalf of the defendant, and that, therefore, he probably meant to suffer the cause to go by default. The court inquired whether any counsel at the bar was instructed to appear for Darbyshire, in the case Shiffnal *v.* Darbyshire, but there was no reply; and learned gentlemen looked at one another, and all shook their learned wigs; and the judge was about to declare that the cause was forfeited by the defendant, John Darbyshire, by non-appearance at the place of trial, when there was seen a bustle near the box of the clerk of the court; there was a hasty plucking off of a large hat, which somebody had apparently walked into court with on; and the moment afterwards a short man, in a Quaker dress, with his grizzled hair hanging in long locks on his shoulders, and smoothed close down on the forehead, stepped, with a peculiar air of confidence and cunning, up to the bar. His tawny, sunburnt features, and small dark eyes, twinkling with an expression of much country subtlety, proclaimed him at once a character. At once a score of voices murmured, — "There's Johnny Darbyshire himself!"

He glanced, with a quick and peculiar look, at the counsel, sitting at their table with their papers before them, who, on their part, did not fail to return his survey with a stare of mixed wonder and amazement. You could see it as plainly as possible written on their faces, — "Who have we got here? There is some fun brewing here, to a certainty."

But Johnny raised his eyes from them to the bench, where sat the judge, and sent them rapidly thence to the jury-box, where they seemed to rest with a considerable satisfaction.

"Is this a witness?" inquired the judge. "If so, what is he doing there, or why does he appear at all, till we know whether the cause is to be defended?"

"Ay, Lord Judge, as they call thee, I reckon I am a witness, and the best witness too, that can be had in the case, for I'm the man himself; I'm John Darbyshire. I didn't mean to have anything to do with these chaps i' their wigs and gowns, with their long, dangling sleeves; and I dunna yet mean to have anything to do wi' 'em. But I just heard one of 'em tell thee, that this cause was not going to be defended; and that put my monkey up, and so, thinks I, I'll e'en up and tell 'em that it will be defended though; ay, and I reckon it will too; Johnny Darbyshire was never yet afraid of the face of any man, or any set of men."

"If you are what you say, good man," said the judge, "defendant in this case, you had better appoint counsel to state it for you."

"Nay, nay, Lord Judge, as they call thee, — hold a bit; I know better than that. Catch Johnny Darbyshire at flinging his money into a lawyer's bag! No, no. I know them chaps wi' wigs well enough. They 've tongues as long as a besom's teal, and fingers as long to poke after 'em. Nay, nay, I don't get my money so easily as to let them scrape it up by armfuls. I 've worked early and late, in heat and cold, for my bit o' money, and long enough too, before these smart chaps had left their mother's apron-strings; and let them catch a coin of it, if they can. No! I know this case better than any other man can, and for why? Because I was in it. It was me that had the mare to summer; it was me that rode her to the doctor; I was in at th' breaking of th' leg, and, for that reason, I can tell you exactly how it all happened. And what 's any of those counsellors, — sharp, and fine, and knowing as they look, with their tails and their powder, — what are they to know about the matter, except what somebody 'd have to tell 'em first? I tell you, I saw it, I did it, and so there needs no twice telling of the story."

"But are you going to produce evidence?" inquired the counsel for the other side.

"Evidence? to be sure I am. What does the chap mean? Evidence? why, I 'm defender and evidence and all!"

There was a good deal of merriment in the court, and at the bar, in which the judge himself joined.

"There wants no evidence besides me; for, as I tell you, I did it, and I'm not going to deny it."

"Stop!" cried the judge; "this is singular. If Mr. Darbyshire means to plead his own cause, and to include in it his evidence, he must be sworn. Let the oath be administered to him."

"Nay, I reckon thou need put none of thy oaths to me! My father never brought me up to cursing and swearing, and such like wickedness. He left that to th' ragamuffins and rapscallions i' th' street. I'm no swearer, nor liar neither, — thou may take my word safe enough."

"Let him take his affirmation, if he be a member of the Society of Friends."

"Ay, now thou speaks sense, Lord Judge. Ay, I'm a member, I warrant me."

The clerk of the court here took his affirmation, and then Johnny proceeded.

"Well, I don't feel myself any better or any honester now for making that affirmation. I was just going to tell the plain truth before, and I can only tell th' same now. And, as I said, I'm not going to deny what I've done. No! Johnny Darbyshire's not the man that ever did a thing and then denied it. Can any of these chaps i' th' wigs say as much? Ay, now I reckon," added he, shaking his head archly at the gentlemen of the bar, "now I reckon you'd like, a good many on you there, to be denying this thing stoutly for me? You'd soon persuade a good many simple folks here that I never did ride the mare, never broke her leg, nay, never saw her that day at all. Wouldn't you, now? wouldn't you?" —

Here the laughter, on all sides, was loudly renewed.

"But I'll take precious good care ye *dunna!* No, no! that's the very thing that I've stepped up here for. It's to keep your consciences clear of a few more additional lies. O dear! I'm quite grieved for you, when I think what falsities and deceit you'll one day have to answer for, as it is."

The gentlemen, thus complimented, appeared to enjoy the satire of Johnny Darbyshire; and still more was it relished in the body of the court.

But again remarked the judge, "Mr. Darbyshire, I advise you to leave the counsel for the plaintiff to prove his case against you."

"I 'st niver oss!" exclaimed Johnny, with indignation.

"I 'st niver oss!" repeated the judge. "What does he mean? — I don't understand him." And he looked inquiringly at the bar.

"He means," my lord, said a young counsel, "that he shall never offer, — never attempt to do so."

"That's a Darbyshire chap now," said Johnny, turning confidentially towards the jury-box, where he saw some of his county farmers. "He understands good English."

"But, good neighbors there," added he, addressing the jury, "for I reckon it's you that I must talk to on this business; I'm glad to see that you are, a good many on you, farmers like myself, and so up to these things. To make a short matter of it, then, — I had the mare and foal to summer; and the gentleman laid it down, strong and fast, that she should n't be ridden by anybody. And I promised him that I would do my best, that nobody should ride her. I told him that I would use her just as if she was my own, — and I meant it. I meant to do the handsome by her and her master too; for I need n't tell you that I 'm too fond of a bit of good blood to see it willingly come to any harm. Nay, nay, that never was the way of Johnny Darbyshire. And there she was, the pretty creature, with her handsome foal cantering and capering round her in the meadow; it was a pleasure to see it, it was indeed! And often have I stood and leaned over the gate and watched them, till I felt a'most as fond of them as of my own children; and never would leg have crossed her while she was in my possession had that not happened that may happen to any man, when he least expects it.

"My wife had been ill, very ill. My poor Lizzy, I thought I should ha' certainly lost her. The doctors said she must be kept quiet in bed; if she stirred for five days she was a lost woman. Well, one afternoon as I was cutting a bit o' grass at th' bottom o' th' orchard for the osses, again they came from ploughing the fallows, I heard a shriek that went through me like a baggonet. Down I flings th' scythe. 'That 's Lizzy, and no other!' I shouted to myself. 'She 's out of bed, — and, goodness! what can it be? She 's ten to one gone mad with a brain fever!' There seemed to have fallen ten thousand millstones on my heart. I tried to run, but I could n't. I was as cold as ice. I was as fast rooted to the ground as a tree. There was another shriek more piercing than before — and I was off like an arrow from a bow — I was loose then. I was all on fire. I ran like a madman till I came within sight of th' house; and there I saw Lizzy in her nightgown with half her body out of the window, shrieking and wringing her hands like any crazed body.

"'Stop! stop!' I cried, 'Lizzy! Lizzy! back! back! for Heaven's sake!'

"'There! there!' screamed she, pointing with staring eyes and ghastly face down into the Darrant that runs under the windows.

"'O God!' I exclaimed, 'she'll drown herself! she's crazed, she means to fling herself in' — groaning as I ran, and trying to keep crying to her, but my voice was dead in my throat.

"When I reached her chamber, I found her fallen on the floor, — she was as white as a ghost, and sure enough I thought she was one. I lifted her upon the bed, and screamed amain for the nurse, for the maid, but not a soul came. I rubbed Lizzy's hands; clapped them; tried her smelling-bottle. At length she came to herself with a dreadful groan, — flashed open her eyes wide on me, and cried, 'Didst see him? Didst save him? Where is he? Where is he?'

"'Merciful Providence!' I exclaimed. 'She's gone only too sure! It's all over with her!'

"'Where is he? Where's my dear Sam? Thou didn't let him drown?'

"'Drown? Sam? What?' I cried. 'What dost mean, Lizzy?'

"'O John! Sammy!—he was drowning i' th' Darrant—oh!—'

"She fainted away again, and a dreadful truth flashed on my mind. She had seen our little Sammy drowning; she had heard his screams, and sprung out of bed, forgetful of herself, and looking out, saw our precious boy in the water. He was sinking! He cried for help! there was nobody near, and there Lizzy stood and saw him going, going, going down! There was not a soul in the house. The maid was gone to see her mother that was dying in the next village; the nurse had been suddenly obliged to run off to the doctor's for some physic; Lizzy had promised to lie still till I came in, and in the mean time—this happens. When I understood her I flew down stairs, and towards the part of the river she had pointed to. I gazed here and there, and at length caught sight of the poor boy's coat floating, and with a rake I caught hold of it, and dragged him to land. But it was too late! Frantic, however, as I was, I flew down to the meadow with a bridle in my hand, mounted the blood mare,—she was the fleetest in the field by half,—and away to the doctor. We went like the wind. I took a short cut for better speed, but it was a hobbly road. Just as I came in sight of the doctor's house there was a slough that had been mended with stones and fagots and anything that came to hand. I pushed her over, but her foot caught in a hole amongst the sticks, and—crack! it was over in a moment.

"Neighbors, neighbors! think of my situation. Think of my feelings. Oh! I was all one great groan! My wife! my boy! the mare! it seemed as if Job's devil was really sent out against me. But there was no time to think; I could only feel, and I could do that running. I sprang over the hedge. I was across the fields, and at the doctor's; ay, long before I could find breath to tell him what was amiss. But he thought it was my wife that was dreadfully worse. 'I expected as much,' said he, and that instant we were in the gig that stood at the door, and we were going like fire back again. But —"

Here Johnny Darbyshire paused; the words stuck in his throat, — his lips trembled, — his face gradually grew pale and livid, as if he were going to give up the ghost. The court was extremely moved: there was a deep silence, and there were heard sobs from the throng behind. The judge sate with his eyes fixed on his book of minutes, and not a voice even said "Go on."

Johnny Darbyshire meantime, overcome by his feelings, had sate down at the bar, a glass of water was handed to him, — he wiped his forehead with his handkerchief several times, heaved a heavy convulsive sigh or two from his laboring chest, — and again arose.

"Judge, then," said he, again addressing the jury, "what a taking I was in. My boy — but no — I canna touch on that, he was — gone!" said he in a husky voice that seemed to require all his physical force to send it from the bottom of his chest. "My wife was for weeks worse than dead, and never has been, and never will be, herself again. When I inquired after the mare, — you can guess — when was a broken leg of a horse successfully set again? They had been obliged to kill her!

"Now, neighbors, I deny nothing. I wunna! — but I'll put it to any of you, if you were in like case, and a fleet mare stood ready at hand, would you have weighed anything but her speed against a wife and — a child? — No, had she been my own, I should have taken her, and that was all I had promised! But there, neighbors, you have the whole business, — and so do just as you like, — I leave it wi' you."

Johnny Darbyshire stepped down from the bar, and disappeared in the crowd. There was a deep silence in the court, and the very jury were seen dashing some drops from their eyes. They appeared to look up to the judge as if they were ready to give in at once their verdict, and nobody could doubt for which party; but at this moment the counsel for the plaintiff arose, and said: —

"Gentlemen of the jury, — you know the old saying — 'He that pleads his own cause has a fool for his client.' We cannot say that the proverb has held good in this case. The defendant has proved himself no fool. Never in my life have I listened to the pleadings of an opponent with deeper anxiety. Nature and the awful chances of life have made the defendant in this case more than eloquent. For a moment I actually trembled for the cause of my client, — but it was for a moment only. I should have been something less than human if I had not, like every person in this court, been strangely affected by the singular appeal of the singular man who has just addressed you; but I should have been something less than a good lawyer if I did not again revert confidently to those facts which were in the possession of my witnesses now waiting to be heard. Had this been the only instance in which the defendant had broken his engagement, and mounted this mare, I should in my own mind have flung off all hope of a verdict from you. God and nature would have been too strong for me in your hearts; but, fortunately for my client, it is not so. I will show you on the most unquestionable evidence that it was not the first nor the second time that Mr. Darbyshire had mounted this prohibited but tempting steed. He had been seen, as one of the witnesses expresses it, 'frisking about' on this beautiful animal, and asking his neighbors what they thought of such a bit of blood as that. He had on one occasion been as far as Crich fair with her, and had allowed her to be cheapened by several dealers as if she were his own, and then proudly rode off, saying, 'Nay, nay, it was not money that would purchase pretty Nancy,' as he called her." Here the counsel called several respectable farmers who amply corroborated these statements; and he then proceeded. "Gentlemen, there I rest my case. You will forget the wife and the child, and call to mind the 'frisking,' and Crich fair. But to put the matter beyond a doubt we will call the defendant again, and put a few questions to him."

The court crier called, — but it was in vain. Johnny Darbyshire was no longer there. As he had said, "he had left it wi' 'em," and was gone. The weight of evidence prevailed; the jury gave a verdict for the plaintiff, — one hundred pounds.

The verdict was given, but the money was not yet got. When called on for payment, Johnny Darbyshire took no further notice of the demand than he had done of the action. An execution was issued against his goods; but when it was served, it was found that he had no goods. A brother stepped in with a clear title to all on Johnny's farm by a deed dated six years before, on plea of moneys advanced, and Johnny stood only as manager.

The plaintiff was so enraged at this barefaced scheme to bar his just claim, Johnny's bail sureties being found equally unsubstantial, that he resolved to arrest Johnny's person. The officers arrived at Johnny's house to serve the writ, and found him sitting at his luncheon alone. It was a fine summer's day, — everybody was out in the fields at the hay. Door and window stood open, and Johnny, who had been out on some business, was refreshing himself before going to the field too. The officers entering declared him their prisoner. "Well," said Johnny, "I know that very well. Don't I know a bum-baily when I see him? But sit down and take something; I 'm hungry if you ar'na, at all events."

The men gladly sate down to a fine piece of cold beef, and Johnny said, "Come, fill your glasses; I 'll fetch another jug of ale. I reckon you 'll not give me a glass of ale like this where we are going."

He took a candle, descended the cellar, one of the officers peeping after him to see that all was right, and again sitting down to the beef and beer. Both of them found the beef splendid; but beginning to find the ale rather long in making its appearance, they descended the cellar, and found Johnny Darbyshire had gone quietly off at a back door.

Loud was the laughter of the country round at Johnny Darbyshire's outwitting of the bailiffs, and desperate was their quest after him. It was many a day, however, before they again got sight of him. When they did, it was on his own hearth, just as they had done at first. Not a soul was visible but himself. The officers declared now that they would make sure of him, and yet drink with him too.

"With all my heart," said Johnny; "and draw it yourselves, too, if you will."

"Nay, I will go down with you," said one; "my comrade shall wait here above."

"Good," said Johnny, lighting a candle.

"Now, mind, young man," added he, going hastily forwards towards the cellar steps, — "mind, I say, some of these steps are bad. It's a dark road, and — nay, here! — this way, — follow me exactly."

But the man was too eager not to let Johnny go too far before him; he did not observe that Johnny went some distance round before he turned down the steps. There was no hand-rail to this dark flight of steps, and he walked straight over into the opening.

"Hold! — hold! Heavens! the man's gone, — did n't I tell him! — "

A heavy plunge and a groan announced the man's descent into the cellar.

"Help! — help!" cried Johnny Darbyshire, rushing wildly into the room above. "The man, like a madman, has walked over the landing into the cellar. If he is n't killed, it's a mercy. Help!" snatching another candle; "but hold — take heed! take heed! or thou 'lt go over after him!"

With good lighting, and careful examination of the way, the officer followed. They found the other man lying on his back, bleeding profusely from his head, and insensible.

"We must have help! there's no time to lose!" cried Johnny Darbyshire, springing up stairs.

"Stop!" cried the distracted officer, left with his bleeding fellow, and springing up the steps after Johnny. But he found a door already bolted in his face; and cursing Johnny for a treacherous and murderous scoundrel, he began vainly denouncing his barbarity in leaving his comrade thus to perish, and kicked and thundered lustily at the door.

But he did Johnny Darbyshire injustice. Johnny had no wish to hurt a hair of any man's head. The officer had been eager and confident, and occasioned his own fall; and even now Johnny had not deserted him. He appeared on horseback at the barn where threshers were at work; told them what had happened; gave them the key of the cellar door, bade them off and help all they could; and said he was riding for the doctor. The doctor indeed soon came, and pronounced the man's life in no danger, though he was greatly scratched and bruised. Johnny himself was again become invisible.

From this time for nine months the pursuit of Johnny Darbyshire was a perfect campaign, full of stratagems, busy marchings, and expectations, but of no surprises. House, barns, fields, and woods, were successively ferreted through, as report whispered that he was in one or the other. But it was to no purpose; not a glimpse of him was ever caught; and fame now loudly declared that he had safely transferred himself to America. Unfortunately for the truth of this report, which had become as well received as the soundest piece of history, Johnny Darbyshire was one fine moonlight night encountered full face to face, by some poachers crossing the fields near his house. The search became again more active than ever, and the ruins of Wingfield Manor, which stood on a hill not far from his dwelling, were speedily suspected to be haunted by him. These were hunted over and over, but no trace of Johnny Darbyshire, or any sufficient hiding-place for him, could be found, till, one fine summer evening, the officers were lucky enough to hit on a set of steps which descended amongst bushes into the lower part of the ruins. Here, going on, they found themselves, to their astonishment, in an ample old kitchen, with a fire of charcoal in the grate, and Johnny Darbyshire with a friend or two sitting most cosily over their tea. Before they could recover from their surprise, Johnny, however, had vanished by some door or window, they could not tell exactly where, for there were sundry doorways issuing into dark places of which former experience bade them beware. Rushing up again, therefore, to the light, they soon posted some of their number around the ruins, and, with other assistance sent for from the village, they descended again, and commenced a vigilant search. This had been patiently waited for a good while by those posted without, when suddenly, as rats are seen to issue from a rick when the ferret is in it, Johnny Darbyshire was seen ascending hurriedly a broken staircase, that was partly exposed to the open day by the progress of dilapidation, and terminated abruptly above.

Here, at this abrupt and dizzy termination, for the

space of half a minute, stood Johnny Darbyshire, looking round, as if calmly surveying the landscape, which lay, with all its greenness and ascending smokes of cottage chimneys, in the gleam of the setting sun. Another instant, and an officer of the law was seen cautiously scrambling up the same ruinous path; but, when he had reached within about half a dozen yards or so of Johnny, he paused, gazed upwards and downwards, and then remained stationary. Johnny, taking one serious look at him, now waved his hand as bidding him adieu, and disappeared in a mass of ivy.

The astonished officer on the ruined stair now hastily retreated downwards; the watchers on the open place around ran to the side of the building where Johnny Darbyshire had thus disappeared, but had scarcely reached the next corner, when they heard a loud descent of stones and rubbish, and, springing forward, saw these rushing to the ground at the foot of the old Manor, and some of them springing and bounding down the hill below. What was most noticeable, however, was Johnny Darbyshire himself, lying stretched, apparently lifeless, on the greensward at some little distance.

On examining afterwards the place, they found that Johnny had descended between a double wall, — a way, no doubt, well known to him, and thence had endeavored to let himself down the wall by the ivy which grew enormously strong there; but the decayed state of the stones had caused the hold of the ivy to give way, and Johnny had been precipitated, probably from a considerable height. He still held quantities of leaves and ivy twigs in his hands.

He was conveyed as speedily as possible on a door to his own house, where it was ascertained by the surgeon that life was sound in him, but that besides plenty of severe contusions, he had broken a thigh. When this news reached his persecutor, though Johnny was declared to have rendered himself, by his resistance to the officers of the law, liable to outlawry, this gentleman declared that he was quite satisfied; that Johnny was punished enough, especially as he had been visited with the very mischief he had occasioned to the mare. He declined to proceed any further against him, paid all charges and costs, and the court itself thought fit to take no further cognizance of the matter.

Johnny was, indeed, severely punished. For nearly twelve months he was confined to the house, and never did his indomitable and masterful spirit exhibit itself so strongly and characteristically as during this time. He was a most troublesome subject in the house. As he sate in his bed, he ordered, scolded, and ruled with a rod of iron all the women, including his wife and daughter, so that they would have thought the leg and the confinement nothing to what they had to suffer.

He at length had himself conveyed to the sitting-room or the kitchen, as he pleased, in a great easy-chair; but as he did not satisfy himself that he was sufficiently obeyed, he one day sent the servant-girl to fetch him the longest scarlet-bean stick that she could find in the garden. Armed with this, he now declared that he would have his own way, — he could reach them now! And, accordingly, there he sate, ordering and scolding, and, if not promptly obeyed in his most extravagant commands, not sparing to inflict substantial knocks with his pea-prick, as he called it. This succeeded so well that he would next have his chair carried to the door, and survey the state of things without.

"Ay, he knew they were going on prettily. There was fine management, he was sure, when he was thus laid up. He should be ruined, that was certain. O, if he could but see the ploughing and the crops, — to see how they were going on would make the heart of a stone ache, he expected."

His son was a steady young fellow, and, it must be known, was all the while farming, and carrying on the business much better than he himself had ever done.

"But he would be with them one of these days, and for the present he would see his stock at all events."

He accordingly ordered the whole of his stock, his horses, his cows, his bullocks, his sheep, his calves, his pigs, and poultry, to be all, every head of them, driven past as he sate at the door. It was like another naming of the beasts by Adam, or another going up into the Ark. There he sate, swaying his long stick, now talking to this horse, and now to that cow. To the old bull he addressed a long speech; and every now and then he broke off to rate the farm-servants for their neglect of things. "What a bag of bones was this heifer! What a skeleton was that horse! Why, they must have been fairly starved on purpose; nay, they must have been in the pinfold all the time he had been laid up. But he would teach the lazy rogues a different lesson as soon as he could get about."

And the next thing was to get about in his cart with his bed laid in it. In this he rode over his farm; and it would have made a fine scene for Fielding or Goldsmith, to have seen all his proceedings, and heard all his exclamations and remarks, as he surveyed field after field.

"What ploughing! what sowing! Why, they must have had a crooked plough, and a set of bandy-legged horses, to plough such ploughing. There was no more straightness in their furrows than in a dog's hind leg. And then where had the man flung the seed to? Here was a bit come up, and there never a bit. It was his belief that they must go to Jericho to find half of his corn that had been flung away. What! had they picked the windiest day of all the year to scatter his corn on the air in? And then the drains were all stopped; the land was drowning, was starving to death; and where were the hedges all gone to? Hedges he left, but now he only saw gaps!"

So he went round the farm, and for many a day did it furnish him with a theme of scolding in the house.

Such was Johnny Darbyshire; and thus he lived for many years. We sketch no imaginary character, we relate no invented story. Perhaps a more perfect specimen of the shrewd and clever man converted into the local and domestic tyrant, by having too much of his own humor, never was beheld; but the genus to which Johnny Darbyshire belonged is far from extinct. In the nooks of England there are not a few of them yet to be found in all their froward glory; and in the most busy cities, though the great prominences of their eccentricities are rubbed off by daily concussion with men as hard-headed as themselves, we see glimpses beneath the polished surface of what they would be in ruder and custom-freer scenes. The Johnny Darbyshires may be said to be instances of English independence run to seed.

THE GRIDIRON.

BY SAMUEL LOVER.

A CERTAIN old gentleman in the west of Ireland, whose love of the ridiculous quite equalled his taste for claret and fox-hunting, was wont, upon festive occasions, when opportunity offered, to amuse his friends by *drawing out* one of his servants, exceedingly fond of what he termed his "thravels," and in whom, a good deal of whim, some queer stories, and perhaps, more than all, long and faithful services, had established a right of loquacity. He was one of those few trusty and privileged domestics, who, if his master unheedingly uttered a rash thing in a fit of passion, would venture to set him right. If the squire said, "I'll turn that rascal off," my friend Pat would say, "Troth you won't, sir"; and Pat was always right, for if any altercation arose upon the "subject-matter in hand," he was sure to throw in some good reason, either from former services, — general good conduct, — or the delinquent's "wife and children," that always turned the scale.

But I am digressing: on such merry meetings as I have alluded to, the master, after making certain "approaches," as a military man would say, as the preparatory steps in laying siege to some *extravaganza* of his servant, might, perchance, assail Pat thus: "By the by, Sir John (addressing a distinguished guest), Pat has a very curious story, which something you told me to-day reminds me of. You remember, Pat (turning to the man, evidently pleased at the notice thus paid to himself), — you remember that queer adventure you had in France?"

"Troth I do, sir," grins forth Pat.

"What!" exclaims Sir John, in feigned surprise, "was Pat ever in France?"

"Indeed he was," cries mine host; and Pat adds, "Ay, and farther, plaze your honor."

"I assure you, Sir John," continues my host, "Pat told me a story once that surprised me very much, respecting the ignorance of the French."

"Indeed!" rejoined the baronet; "really, I always supposed the French to be a most accomplished people."

"Troth, then, they 're not, sir," interrupts Pat.

"O, by no means," adds mine host, shaking his head emphatically.

"I believe, Pat, 't was when you were crossing the Atlantic?" says the master, turning to Pat with a seductive air, and leading into the "full and true account" — (for Pat had thought fit to visit *North Amerikay*, for "a raison he had," in the autumn of the year ninety-eight).

"Yes, sir," says Pat, "the broad Atlantic," — a favorite phrase of his, which he gave with a brogue as broad, almost, as the Atlantic itself.

"It was the time I was lost in crassin' the broad Atlantic, a comin' home," began Pat, decoyed into the recital; "whin the winds began to blow, and the sae to rowl, that you 'd think the *Colleen Dhas* (that was her name), would not have a mast left but what would rowl out of her.

"Well, sure enough, the masts went by the board, at last, and the pumps were choked (divil choke them for that same), and av coorse the water gained an us; and troth, to be filled with water is neither good for man or baste; and she was sinkin' fast, settlin' down, as the sailors call it; and faith I never was good at settlin' down in my life, and I liked it then less nor ever; accordingly we prepared for the worst and put out the boat and got a sack o' bishkits and a cask o' pork, and a kag o' wather, and a thrifle o' rum aboord, and any other little matthers we could think iv in the mortial hurry we wor in, — and faith there was no time to be lost, for, my darlint, the *Colleen Dhas* went down like a lump o' lead, afore we wor many sthrokes o' the oar away from her.

"Well, we dhrifted away all that night, and next mornin' we put up a blanket an the end av a pole as well as we could, and then we sailed iligant; for we dar n't show a stitch o' canvas the night before, bekase it was blowin' like bloody murther, savin' your presence, and sure it 's the wondher of the world we wor n't swally'd alive by the ragin' sae.

"Well, away we wint, for more nor a week, and nothin' before our two good-lookin' eyes but the canophy iv heaven, and the wide ocean — the broad Atlantic — not a thing was to be seen but the sae and the sky; and though the sae and the sky is mighty purty things in themselves, throth they 're no great things when you 've nothin' else to look at for a week together, — and the barest rock in the world, so it was land, would be more welkim. And then, soon enough, throth, our provisions began to run low, the bishkits, and the wather, and the rum — throth *that* was gone first of all — God help uz — and oh! it was thin that starvation began to stare us in the face, — 'O, murther, murther, Captain darlint,' says I, 'I wish we could land anywhere,' says I.

"'More power to your elbow, Paddy, my boy,' says he, 'for sitch a good wish, and throth it's myself wishes the same.'

"'Och,' says I, 'that it may plaze you, sweet queen iv heaven, supposing it was only a *dissolute* island,' says I, 'inhabited wid Turks, sure they wouldn't be such bad Christians as to refuse us a bit and a sup.'

"'Whisht, whisht, Paddy,' says the captain, 'don't be talking bad of any one,' says he; 'you don't know how soon you may want a good word put in for yourself, if you should be called to quarthers in th' other world all of a suddint,' says he.

"'Thrue for you, Captain darlint,' says I — I called him darlint, and made free with him, you see, bekase disthress makes us all equal, — 'thrue for you, Captain jewel, — God betune uz and harm, I owe no man any spite, — and throth that was only thruth. Well, the last bishkit was sarved out, and by gor the *wather itself* was all gone at last, and we passed the night mighty cowld; well, at the brake o' day the sun riz most beautifully out

N

o' the waves, that was as bright as silver and as clear as chrystal. But it was only the more cruel upon us, for we wor beginnin' to feel *terrible* hungry; when all at wanst I thought I spied the land, — by gor, I thought I felt my heart up in my throat in a minit, and 'Thunder an' turf, Captain,' says I, 'look to leeward,' says I.

"'What for?' says he.

"'I think I see the land,' says I. So he ups with his bring-'em-near (that's what the sailors call a spy-glass, sir), and looks out, and, sure enough, it was.

"'Hurra!' says he, 'we're all right now; pull away, my boys,' says he.

"'Take care you're not mistaken,' says I; 'maybe it's only a fog-bank, Captain darlint,' says I.

"'O no,' says he, 'it's the land in airnest.'

"'O, then, whereabouts in the wide world are we, Captain?' says I; 'maybe it id be in *Roosia*, or *Proosia*, or the Garmant Oceant,' says I.

"'Tut, you fool,' says he, for he had that consaited way wid him — thinkin' himself cleverer nor any one else — 'tut, you fool,' says he, 'that's *France*,' says he.

"'Tare an ouns,' says I, 'do you tell me so? and how do you know it's France it is, Captain dear,' says I.

"'Bekase this is the Bay o' Bishky we're in now,' says he.

"'Throth, I was thinkin' so myself,' says I, 'by the rowl it has; for I often heerd av it in regard of that same; and throth the likes av it I never seen before nor since, and, with the help of God, never will.'

"Well, with that, my heart began to grow light; and when I seen my life was safe, I began to grow twice hungrier nor ever — so, says I, 'Captain jewel, I wish we had a gridiron.'

"'Why, then,' says he, 'thunder and turf,' says he, 'what puts a gridiron into your head?'

"'Bekase I 'm starvin' with the hunger,' says I.

"'And sure, bad luck to you,' says he, 'you could n't eat a gridiron,' says he, 'barrin' you were a *pelican o' the wildherness*,' says he.

"'Ate a gridiron,' says I, 'och, in throth, I 'm not such a *gommoch* all out as that, anyhow. But sure, if we had a gridiron, we could dress a beefstake,' says I.

"'Arrah! but where 's the beefstake?' says he.

"'Sure, could n't we cut a slice aff the pork,' says I.

"'Be gor, I never thought o' that,' says the captain. 'You 're a clever fellow, Paddy,' says he, laughin'.

"'O, there 's many a thrue word said in joke,' says I.

"'Thrue for you, Paddy,' says he.

"'Well, then,' says I, 'if you put me ashore there beyant' (for we were nearin' the land all the time), 'and sure I can ax them for to lind me the loan of a gridiron,' says I.

"'O, by gor, the butther 's comin' out o' the stirabout in airnest now,' says he, 'you gommoch,' says he, 'sure I told you before that 's France, — and sure they 're all furriners there,' says the captain.

"'Well,' says I, 'and how do you know but I 'm as good a furriner myself as any o' thim?'

"'What do you mane?' says he.

"'I mane,' says I, 'what I towld you, that I 'm as good a furriner myself as any o' thim.'

"'Make me sinsible,' says he.

"'By dad, maybe that's more nor me, or greater nor me, could do,' says I, — and we all began to laugh at him, for I thought I would pay him off for his bit o' consait about the Garmant Oceant.

"'Lave aff your humbuggin',' says he, 'I bid you, and tell me what it is you mane, at all at all.'

"'*Parly voo frongsay*,' says I.

"'O, your humble sarvant,' says he; 'why, by gor, you're a scholar, Paddy.'

"'Throth, you may say that,' says I.

"'Why, you're a clever fellow, Paddy,' says the captain, jeerin' like.

"'You're not the first that said that,' says I, 'whether you joke or no.'

"'O, but I'm in airnest,' says the captain; 'and do you tell me, Paddy,' says he, 'that you spake Frinch?'

"'*Parly voo frongsay*,' says I.

"'By gor, that bangs Banagher, and all the world knows Banagher bangs the divil, — I never met the likes o' you, Paddy,' says he, — 'pull away, boys, and put Paddy ashore, and maybe we won't get a good bellyful before long.'

"So, with that, it wos no sooner said nor done, — they pulled away, and got close into shore in less than no time, and run the boat up in a little creek, and a beautiful creek it was, with a lovely white sthrand, — an illegant place for ladies to bathe in the summer; and out I got, — and it's stiff enough in the limbs I was, afther bein' cramped up in the boat, and perished with the cowld and hunger, but I conthrived to scramble on, one way or t' other, tow'rds a little bit iv a wood that was close to the shore, and the smoke curlin' out iv it, quite timptin' like.

"'By the powdhers o' war, I'm all right,' says I, 'there's a house there,'—and sure enough there was, and a parcel of men, women, and childher, ating their dinner round a table, quite convanient. And so I wint up to the door, and I thought I'd be very civil to them, as I heerd the French was always mighty p'lite intirely, —and I thought I'd show them I knew what good manners was.

"So I took aff my hat, and, making a low bow, says I, 'God save all here,' says I.

"Well, to be sure, they all stapt eating at wanst, and began to stare at me, and faith they almost looked me out of countenance,—and I thought to myself, it was not good manners at all, more betoken from furriners which they call so mighty p'lite; but I never minded that, in regard o' wantin' the gridiron; and so says I, 'I beg your pardon,' says I, 'for the liberty I take, but it's only bein' in disthress in regard of eating,' says I, 'that I made bowld to throuble yez, and if you could lind me the loan of a gridiron,' says I, 'I'd be entirely oblceged to ye.'

"By gor, they all stared at me twice worse nor before, —and with that, says I (knowing what was in their minds), 'Indeed it's thrue for you,' says I, 'I'm tatthered to pieces, and God knows I look quare enough, —but it's by raison of the storm,' says I, 'which dhruv us ashore here below, and we're all starvin',' says I.

"So then they began to look at each other again; and myself, seeing at once dirty thoughts was in their heads, and that they tuk me for a poor beggar coming to crave charity, — with that, says I, 'O, not at all,' says I, 'by no manes, — we have plenty of mate ourselves there below, and we'll dhress it,' says I, 'if you would be plased to lind us the loan of a gridiron,' says I, makin' a low bow.

"Well, sir, with that, throth, they stared at me twice worse nor ever, and faith I began to think that maybe the captain was wrong, and that it was not France at all at all; and so says I, 'I beg pardon, sir,' says I, to a fine ould man, with a head of hair as white as silver, — 'maybe I'm under a mistake,' says I, 'but I thought I was in France, sir: are n't you furriners?' says I, — '*Parly voo frongsay?*'

"'We, munseer,' says he.

"'Then would you lind me the loan of a gridiron,' says I, 'if you plase?'

"O, it was thin that they started at me as if I had seven heads; and, faith, myself began to feel flushed like and onaisy, — and so, says I, makin' a bow and scrape agin, 'I know it's a liberty I take, sir,' says I, 'but it's only in the regard of bein' cast away; and if you plase, sir,' says I, '*parly voo frongsay?*'

"'We, munseer,' says he, mighty sharp.

"'Then would you lend me the loan of a gridiron!' says I, 'and you'll obleege me.'

"Well, sir, the ould chap began to munseer me; but the devil a bit of a gridiron he'd gi' me; and so I began to think they wor all neygars, for all their fine manners; and throth my blood begun to rise, and says I, 'By my sowl, if it was you was in distress,' says I, 'and if it was to ould Ireland you kem, it's not only the gridiron they'd give you, if you axed it, but something to put an it, too, and the drop o' dhrink into the bargain, and *cead mile failte.*'

"Well, the word *cead mile failte* seemed to sthreck his heart, and the ould chap cocked his ear, and so I thought I'd give him another offer, and make him sensible at last: and so says I, wanst more, quite slow, that he might understand, — 'Parly — voo — frongsay, munseer.'

"'We, munseer,' says he.

"'Then lind me the loan of a gridiron,' says I, 'and bad scram to you.'

"Well, bad win to the bit of it he'd gi' me, and the ould chap begins bowin' and scrapin', and said something or other about a long tongs.*

"'Phoo! — the divil swape yourself and your tongs,' says I, 'I don't want a tongs at all at all; but can't you listen to raison,' says I, — '*Parly voo frongsay?*'

"'We, munseer.'

"'Then lind me the loan of a gridiron,' says I, 'and howld your prate.'

"Well, what would you think, but he shook his old noddle as much as to say he would n't; and so, says I, 'Bad cess to the likes o' that I ever seen, — throth if you wor in my counthry it's not that away they'd use you. The curse o' the crows an you, you owld sinner,' says I, 'the divil a longer I'll darken your door.'

"So he seen I was vexed, and I thought, as I was

---

* Some mystification of Paddy's touching the French *n'entends.*

turnin' away, I seen him begin to relint, and that his conscience throubled him; and says I, turnin' back, 'Well, I'll give one chance more, — you ould thief, — are you a Chrishthan at all? are you a furriner!' says I, 'that all the world calls so p'lite? Bad luck to you, do you understand your own language?—*Parly roo frongsay?*" says I.

"'We, munseer,' says he.

"'Then, thunder an' turf,' says I, 'will you lind me the loan of a gridiron?'

"Well, sir, the devil resave the bit of it he'd gi' me, — and so, with that, the 'curse o' the hungry an you, you ould negarly villain,' says I; 'the back o' my hand and the sowl o' my foot to you, that you may want a gridiron yourself yit,' says I; and with that I left them there, sir, and kem away, — and, in throth, it's often sense that I thought that it was remarkable."

THE BOX TUNNEL.

BY CHARLES READE.

THE 10.15 train glided from Paddington, May 7, 1847. In the left compartment of a certain first-class carriage were four passengers; of these, two were worth description. The lady had a smooth, white, delicate brow, strongly marked eyebrows, long lashes, eyes that seemed to change color, and a good-sized delicious mouth, with teeth as white as milk. A man could not see her nose for her eyes and mouth; her own sex could and would have told us some nonsense about it. She wore an unpretending grayish dress buttoned to the throat with lozenge-shaped buttons, and a Scottish shawl that agreeably evaded color. She was like a duck, so tight her plain feathers fitted her, and there she sat, smooth, snug, and delicious, with a book in her hand, and a *soupçon* of her wrist just visible as she held it. Her opposite neighbor was what I call a good style of man, — the more to his credit, since he belonged to a corporation that frequently turns out the worst imaginable style of young men. He was a cavalry officer, aged twenty-five. He had a mustache, but not a very repulsive one; not one of those subnasal pigtails on which soup is suspended like dew on a shrub; it was short, thick, and black as a coal. His teeth had not yet been turned by tobacco smoke to the color of juice, his clothes did not stick to nor hang to him; he had an engaging smile, and, what I liked the dog for, his vanity, which was inordinate, was in its proper place, his heart, not in his face, jostling mine and other people's who have none, — in a word, he was what one oftener hears of than meets, — a young gentleman. He was conversing in an animated whisper with a companion, a fellow-officer; they were talking about what it is far better not to — women. Our friend clearly did not wish to be overheard; for he cast ever and anon a furtive glance at his fair *vis-à-vis* and lowered his voice. She seemed completely absorbed in her book, and that reassured him. At last the two soldiers came down to a whisper (the truth must be told), the one who got down at Slough, and was lost to posterity, bet ten pounds to three, that he who was going down with us to Bath and immortality would not kiss either of the ladies opposite upon the road. "Done, done!" Now I am sorry a man I have hitherto praised should have lent himself, even in a whisper, to such a speculation; "but nobody is wise at all hours," not even when the clock is striking five and twenty; and you are to consider his profession, his good looks, and the temptation — ten to three.

After Slough the party was reduced to three; at Twyford one lady dropped her handkerchief; Captain Dolignan fell on it like a lamb; two or three words were interchanged on this occasion. At Reading the Marlborough of our tale made one of the safe investments of that day, he bought a Times and Punch; the latter full of steel-pen thrusts and woodcuts. Valor and beauty deigned to laugh at some inflamed humbug or other punctured by Punch. Now laughing together thaws our human ice; long before Swindon it was a talking match — at Swindon who so devoted as Captain Dolignan? — he handed them out — he souped them — he tough-chickened them — he brandied and cochinealed one, and he brandied and burnt-sugared the other; on their return to the carriage, one lady passed into the inner compartment to inspect a certain gentleman's seat on that side of the line.

Reader, had it been you or I, the beauty would have been the deserter, the average one would have stayed with us till all was blue, ourselves included; not more surely does our slice of bread and butter, when it escapes from our hand, revolve it ever so often, alight face downward on the carpet. But this was a bit of a fop, Adonis, dragoon, — so Venus remained in *tête-à-tête* with him. You have seen a dog meet an unknown female of his species; how handsome, how *empressé*, how expressive he becomes; such was Dolignan after Swindon, and to do the dog justice, he got handsome and handsomer; and you have seen a cat conscious of approaching cream, — such was Miss Haythorn; she became demurer and demurer; presently our captain looked out of the window and laughed; this elicited an inquiring look from Miss Haythorn.

"We are only a mile from the Box Tunnel."

"Do you always laugh a mile from the Box Tunnel?" said the lady.

"Invariably."

"What for?"

"Why, hem! it is a gentleman's joke."

Captain Dolignan then recounted to Miss Haythorn the following: —

"A lady and her husband sat together going through the Box Tunnel, — there was one gentleman opposite; it was pitch dark: after the tunnel the lady said, 'George, how absurd of you to salute me going through the tunnel.' 'I did no such thing.' 'You did n't?' 'No! why?' 'Because somehow I thought you did!'"

Here Captain Dolignan laughed and endeavored to lead his companion to laugh, but it was not to be done. The train entered the tunnel.

Miss Haythorn. Ah!

Dolignan. What is the matter?

Miss Haythorn. I am frightened.

Dolignan (moving to her side). Pray do not be alarmed; I am near you.

Miss Haythorn. You are near me, — very near me, indeed, Captain Dolignan.

Dolignan. You know my name?

Miss Haythorn. I heard you mention it. I wish we were out of this dark place.

Dolignan. I could be content to spend hours here, reassuring you, my dear lady.

Miss Haythorn. Nonsense!

Dolignan. Pweep! (Grave reader, do not put your

lips to the next pretty creature you meet, or you will understand what this means.)

Miss Haythorn. Ee! Ee!

Friend. What is the matter?

Miss Haythorn. Open the door! Open the door!

There was a sound of hurried whispers, the door was shut and the blind pulled down with hostile sharpness.

If any critic falls on me for putting inarticulate sounds in a dialogue as above, I answer with all the insolence I can command at present. "Hit boys as big as yourself"; bigger, perhaps, such as Sophocles, Euripides, and Aristophanes; they began it, and I learned it of them, sore against my will.

Miss Haythorn's scream lost most of its effect because the engine whistled forty thousand murders at the same moment; and fictitious grief makes itself heard when real cannot.

Between the tunnel and Bath our young friend had time to ask himself whether his conduct had been marked by that delicate reserve which is supposed to distinguish the perfect gentleman.

With a long face, real or feigned, he held open the door; his late friends attempted to escape on the other side,—impossible! they must pass him. She whom he had insulted (Latin for kissed) deposited somewhere at his feet a look of gentle, blushing reproach; the other, whom he had not insulted, darted red-hot daggers at him from her eyes; and so they parted.

It was, perhaps, fortunate for Dolignan that he had the grace to be a friend to Major Hoskyns of his regiment, a veteran laughed at by the youngsters, for the Major was too apt to look coldly upon billiard-balls and cigars; he had seen cannon-balls and linstocks. He had also, to tell the truth, swallowed a good bit of the mess-room poker, which made it as impossible for Major Hoskyns to descend to an ungentlemanlike word or action as to brush his own trousers below the knee.

Captain Dolignan told this gentleman his story in gleeful accents; but Major Hoskyns heard him coldly, and as coldly answered that he had known a man to lose his life for the same thing.

"That is nothing," continued the Major, "but unfortunately he deserved to lose it."

At this, blood mounted to the younger man's temples; and his senior added, "I mean to say he was thirty-five; you, I presume, are twenty-one!"

"Twenty-five."

"That is much the same thing; will you be advised by me?"

"If you will advise me."

"Speak to no one of this, and send White the £3, that he may think you have lost the bet."

"That is hard, when I won it."

"Do it, for all that, sir."

Let the disbelievers in human perfectibility know that this dragoon capable of a blush did this virtuous action, albeit with violent reluctance; and this was his first damper. A week after these events he was at a ball. He was in that state of factitious discontent which belongs to us amiable English. He was looking in vain for a lady, equal in personal attraction to the idea he had formed of George Dolignan as a man, when suddenly there glided past him a most delightful vision! a lady whose beauty and symmetry took him by the eyes,— another look: "It can't be! Yes, it is!" Miss Haythorn! (not that he knew her name!) but what an apotheosis!

The duck had become a peahen — radiant, dazzling, she looked twice as beautiful and almost twice as large as before. He lost sight of her. He found her again. She was so lovely she made him ill — and he, alone, must not dance with her, speak to her. If he had been content to begin her acquaintance the usual way, it might have ended in kissing: it must end in nothing. As she danced, sparks of beauty fell from her on all around, but him — she did not see him; it was clear she never would see him — one gentleman was particularly assiduous; she smiled on his assiduity; he was ugly, but she smiled on him. Dolignan was surprised at his success, his ill taste, his ugliness, his impertinence. Dolignan at last found himself injured; "who was this man? and what right had he to go on so? He never kissed her, I suppose," said Dolle. Dolignan could not prove it, but he felt that somehow the rights of property were invaded. He went home and dreamed of Miss Haythorn, and hated all the ugly successful. He spent a fortnight trying to find out who his beauty was,— he never could encounter her again. At last he heard of her in this way: A lawyer's clerk paid him a little visit and commenced a little action against him in in the name of Miss Haythorn, for insulting her in a railway train.

The young gentleman was shocked; endeavored to soften the lawyer's clerk; that machine did not thoroughly comprehend the meaning of the term. The lady's name, however, was at last revealed by this untoward incident; from her name to her address was but a short step; and the same day our crestfallen hero lay in wait at her door, and many a succeeding day, without effect. But one fine afternoon she issued forth quite naturally, as if she did it every day, and walked briskly on the parade. Dolignan did the same, met and passed her many times on the parade, and searched for pity in her eyes, but found neither look nor recognition, nor any other sentiment; for all this she walked and walked, till all the other promenaders were tired and gone, — then her culprit summoned resolution, and, taking off his hat, with a voice for the first time tremulous, besought permission to address her. She stopped, blushed, and neither acknowledged nor disowned his acquaintance. He blushed, stammered out how ashamed he was, how he deserved to be punished, how he was punished, how little she knew how unhappy he was, and concluded by begging her not to let all the world know the disgrace of a man who was already mortified enough by the loss of her acquaintance. She asked an explanation; he told her of the action that had been commenced in her name; she gently shrugged her shoulders and said, "How stupid they are!" Emboldened by this, he begged to know whether or not a life of distant unpretending devotion would, after a lapse of years, erase the memory of his madness — his crime!

"She did not know!"

"She must now bid him adieu, as she had some preparations to make for a ball in the Crescent, where everybody was to be." They parted, and Dolignan determined to be at the ball, where everybody was to be. He was there, and after some time he obtained an introduction to Miss Haythorn, and he danced with her. Her manner was gracious. With the wonderful tact of her sex, she seemed to have commenced the acquaintance that evening. That night, for the first time, Dolignan was in love. I will spare the reader all a lover's arts, by which he succeeded in dining where she dined, in dancing where she danced, in overtaking her by accident when she rode. His devotion followed her to church, where the dragoon was rewarded by learning there is a world where they neither polk nor smoke, — the two capital abominations of this one.

He made an acquaintance with her uncle, who liked him, and he saw at last with joy that her eye loved to dwell upon him, when she thought he did not observe her. It was three months after the Box Tunnel that Captain Dolignan called one day upon Captain Haythorn, R. N., whom he had met twice in his life, and slightly propitiated by violently listening to a cutting-out expedition; he called, and in the usual way asked permission to pay his addresses to his daughter. The worthy Captain straightway began doing quarter-deck, when suddenly he was summoned from the apartment by a mysterious message. On his return he announced with a total change of voice, that "It was all right, and his visitor might run alongside as soon as he chose." My reader has divined the truth; this nautical commander, terrible to the foe, was in complete and happy subjugation to his daughter, our heroine.

As he was taking leave, Dolignan saw his divinity glide into the drawing-room. He followed her, observed a sweet consciousness deepen into confusion, — she tried to laugh, and cried instead, and then she smiled again; when he kissed her hand at the door it was "George" and "Marian" instead of "Captain" this and "Miss" the other.

A reasonable time after this (for my tale is merciful and skips formalities and torturing delays), these two were very happy; they were once more upon the railroad, going to enjoy their honeymoon all by themselves. Marian Dolignan was dressed just as before, — duck-like and delicious; all bright except her clothes; but George sat beside her this time instead of opposite; and she drank him in gently from her long eyelashes.

"Marian," said George, "married people should tell each other all. Will you ever forgive me if I own to you; no — "

"Yes! yes!"

"Well, then, you remember the Box Tunnel." (This was the first allusion he had ventured to it.) "I am ashamed to say I had £3 to £10 with White I would kiss one of you two ladies," and George, pathetic externally, chuckled within.

"I know that, George; I overheard you," was the demure reply.

"Oh! you overheard me! impossible."

"And did you not hear me whisper to my companion? I made a bet with her."

"You made a bet! how singular! What was it?"

"Only a pair of gloves, George."

"Yes, I know; but what about it?"

"That if you did you should be my husband, dearest."

"Oh! but stay; then you could not have been so very angry with me, love. Why, dearest, then you brought that action against me?"

Mrs. Dolignan looked down.

"I was afraid you were forgetting me! George, you will never forgive me?"

"Sweet angel! why, here is the Box Tunnel!"

Now, reader, — fie! no! no such thing! you can't expect to be indulged in this way every time we come to a dark place. Besides, it is not the thing. Consider, two sensible married people. No such phenomenon, I assure you, took place. No scream in hopeless rivalry of the engine — this time!

www.ingramcontent.com/pod-product-compliance
Lightning Source LLC
Chambersburg PA
CBHW021832230426
43669CB00008B/947